HOW to

READ

the

BIBLE

as

LITERATURE

...and get more
out of it

HOW to
READ
the
BIBLE
as
LITERATURE
...and get more
out of it

LELAND RYKEN

ZONDERVAN™

GRAND RAPIDS, MICHIGAN 49530 USA

We want to hear from you. Please send your comments about this
book to us in care of the address below. Thank you.

GRAND RAPIDS, MICHIGAN 49530 USA

WWW.ZONDERVAN.COM

ZONDERVAN™

How to Read the Bible as Literature
Copyright © 1984 by Zondervan

Requests for information should be addressed to:
Zondervan, *Grand Rapids, Michigan 49530*

Library of Congress Cataloging-in-Publication Data

Ryken, Leland.
    How to read the Bible as literature.
        p. cm.
    Includes index.
    ISBN 0-310-39021-4
    1. Bible as literature.   2. Bible — Criticism, interpretation, etc.   .   I. Title.
BS535.R89 1984
220.6'6   84-19667

Edited by Ed van der Maas
Designed by Louise Bauer

Printed in the United States of America

04 05 06 07 08 /DC/ 32 31 30 29 28 27 26 25

For my parents

Contents

Preface

The one thing the Bible is *not* is what it is so often thought to be—a theological outline with proof texts attached.

Asked to define *neighbor,* Jesus told a story (Luke 10:25–27). Likewise, Jesus' aphoristic command "Remember Lot's wife" (Luke 17:32) shows that he believed that truth can be embodied in concrete examples or images as well as in moral propositions.

When asked by his disciples why he spoke in parables, Jesus outlined a theory of communication (Matt. 13:10–17) based on the literary principle of indirection: he concealed the truth from immediate perception in order to reveal it to listeners who were willing to ponder his parables. Instances from the life of Jesus such as these suggest a literary approach to truth that frequently avoids direct propositional statement and embodies truth in distinctly literary forms.

Furthermore, there is a preoccupation among biblical writers with artistry, verbal craftsmanship, and aesthetic beauty. The writer of Ecclesiastes presents a theory of writing that stresses beauty of expression as well as truthfulness of content; he labored to arrange proverbs "with great care" and "sought to find pleasing words" (Eccl. 12:9–10 RSV). If the Bible is an artistically beautiful as well as a truthful book, it demands a literary approach in addition to the historical and theological approaches.

Traditionally, we have been so preoccupied with the hermeneutical question of how to *interpret* what the Bible says that we have been left impoverished in techniques to *describe* and interact with the text itself. In the thirteenth century, Roger Bacon argued that the church had done a good job of communicating the theological content of the Bible but had failed to make the literal level of the biblical text come alive in people's imaginations. We are in a similar situation today, even though the literary emphasis on the primary or literal level of a biblical text actually builds upon the grammatico-historical method of interpretation, which likewise aims to take a reader as close as possible to the originally intended, plain meaning of the text.

This book is an introduction to the literary forms of the Bible, with emphasis on the activities that those forms require of a reader.

It is a "grammar" of literary forms and techniques. As such, it is a companion or supplement to similar handbooks by biblical scholars.

I am happy for this occasion to thank my Wheaton College colleagues Alan Johnson of the Bible Department and Jim Wilhoit of the Christian Education Department for their unfailing helpfulness in pointing me to material from their disciplines and in sparing me from errors of ignorance. This book also benefited from criticism by Ron Allen of Western Conservative Baptist Seminary and Stanley Gundry, Editor-in-Chief at Zondervan. I am equally indebted to my wife, Mary, for serving as stylistic critic and proofreader.

I have taken most of my biblical quotations from the New International Version. Where I have used the King James Version (KJ) or the Revised Standard Version (RSV), I have so indicated.

Chapter One

Is the Bible Literature?

THERE IS A QUIET REVOLUTION GOING ON in the study of
the Bible. At its center is a growing awareness that
the Bible is a work of literature and that the
methods of literary scholarship are a necessary part
of any complete study of the Bible. There are two
sides to the movement: literary scholars are showing increasing interest in applying their methods to
the Bible, and Bible scholars are calling for a
literary approach.[1]

New Directions
in Biblical
Studies

A number of ingredients make up this new
approach to the Bible: a concern with the literary
genres of the Bible; a new willingness to treat
biblical texts as finished wholes instead of as a
patchwork of fragments; a focus on the Bible as it
now stands instead of conducting excavations in
the redaction (editing) process behind the text; an
inclination to use literary instead of traditional
theological terms to discuss the stories and poems
of the Bible; an appreciation for the artistry of the
Bible; a sensitivity to the experiential, extra-intel-
lectual (more-than-ideational) dimension of the
Bible.

But above all, the new attitude toward the Bible
involves a growing awareness that literature expresses truth in its own way, different from ordinary propositional discourse. In other words, when
the Bible employs a literary method, it asks to be

Approaching
the Bible as
Literature

[1]For selected examples, see the sources listed in the
"Further Reading" section at the end of this chapter.

approached as literature and not as something else. In the words of C. S. Lewis, "There is a . . . sense in which the Bible, since it is after all literature, cannot properly be read except as literature; and the different parts of it as the different sorts of literature they are."[2]

Defining the Term "Literature"

The purpose of this opening chapter is to identify what makes a text "literature." I should say at once that by the term "literature" I do not mean everything that is written. I use it in a more restricted sense to mean the types of writing that are often called "imaginative literature" or "creative writing," in contrast to expository writing. In this chapter, I am in effect defining those parts of the Bible that are like the works covered in high school and college literature courses.

The Literary Continuum

By thus defining literature I am not establishing an "either–or" method of distinguishing between literary and nonliterary texts. The Bible is obviously a mixed book. Literary and nonliterary (expository, explanatory) writing exist side by side within the covers of this unique book. I have no intention of building a "great divide" that would make a biblical passage either literature or nonliterature. Instead, I am describing a continuum, or scale, on which some parts of the Bible are more literary and other parts are less literary.

More Than One Approach Is Necessary

Nor do I wish to suggest that the literary parts of the Bible cannot be approached in other ways as well. I do not question that the literary parts can and should also be approached as history and theology. My claim is simply that the literary approach is one necessary way to read and interpret the Bible, an approach that has been unjustifiably neglected.

Building on Biblical Scholarship

Despite that neglect, the literary approach builds at every turn on what biblical scholars have done to recover the original, intended meaning of the biblical text. In fact, the literary approach that I describe in this book is a logical extension of what is commonly known as the grammatico-historical method of biblical interpretation. Both approaches insist that we must begin with the literal meaning of

---

[2]*Reflections on the Psalms* (New York: Harcourt, Brace and World, 1958), 3.

the words of the Bible as determined by the historical setting in which the authors wrote.

The best way into the subject is to look at a couple of examples. One of the most memorable passages in the whole Bible is the parable Jesus told when a lawyer asked him to define who his neighbor was. Here is the definition of "neighbor" that Jesus gave (Luke 10:30–36):

The Parable of the Good Samaritan

> A man was going down from Jerusalem to Jericho, when he fell into the hands of robbers. They stripped him of his clothes, beat him and went away, leaving him half dead. A priest happened to be going down the same road, and when he saw the man, he passed by on the other side. So too, a Levite, when he came to the place and saw him, passed by on the other side. But a Samaritan, as he traveled, came where the man was; and when he saw him, he took pity on him. He went to him and bandaged his wounds, pouring on oil and wine. Then he put the man on his own donkey, took him to an inn and took care of him. The next day he took out two silver coins and gave them to the innkeeper. "Look after him," he said, "and when I return, I will reimburse you for any extra expense you may have." Which of these three do you think was a neighbor to the man who fell into the hands of robbers?

Everything about this passage makes it a piece of literature. We should notice first that Jesus never gives an abstract or propositional definition of "neighbor." Instead, he tells a story that embodies what it means to *be* a neighbor. This suggests at once the most important thing about literature: its subject matter is human experience, not abstract ideas. Literature *incarnates* its meanings as concretely as possible. The knowledge that literature gives of a subject is the kind of knowledge that is obtained by (vicariously) living through an experience. Jesus could have defined *neighbor* abstractly, as a dictionary does, but he chose a literary approach to the truth instead. This is comparable to an experience we probably have all had when struggling with the assembly of a toy or appliance: when we have a good picture, we may not even need the written instructions.

The Incarnational Nature of Literature

The Primacy of Imagination (Image-Making)

Because literature *presents* an experience instead of telling us *about* that experience, it constantly appeals to our imagination (the image-making and image-perceiving capacity within us). Literature *images forth* some aspect of reality. Consider all the sensory images and gestures we encounter in this parable: robbers stripping and beating a victim on a road, specific people traveling down the road, first-aid equipment consisting of such tangibles as oil and wine, and such physical things as a donkey and an inn and money. We visualize the Samaritan lifting the victim onto his donkey and see the money exchange hands and listen to the instructions at the inn.

The Genre of Story

The form of the parable is as literary as the content is. For one thing, it is a story or narrative, and this is a distinctly literary genre ("type"). The story, moreover, is told with an abundance of literary artistry. It follows the storytelling principle of threefold repetition: a given event happens three times, with a crucial change introduced the third time. The story begins with vivid plot conflict to seize the listener's attention, and from the very start the story generates suspense about its outcome. Jesus also makes skillful use of foils (contrasts that "set off" or heighten the main point of the story): the neighborliness of the Samaritan stands out all the more clearly by its contrast with the indifference of the priest and of the Levite.

Unity, Coherence, Emphasis

Well-constructed stories have unity, coherence, and emphasis. Judged by these artistic criteria, this parable of Jesus is a small masterpiece. Nothing is extraneous to the unifying theme of neighborly behavior from an unlikely source. The very construction of the story makes the emphasis fall on the good Samaritan. One critic describes it thus:

> The aborted sequences with the priest and Levite provide a pattern which causes the listener to anticipate the third traveler and build up tension. Since this threefold pattern is so common in popular story telling, we also anticipate that the third traveler will be the one who will actually help. Our attention is focused on the third traveler before he arrives, and this heightens the shock when we discover that he neither fits the pattern of cultural

expectation nor the pattern of expectation created by the series of priest, Levite.[3]

Not only is the parable inherently literary; its effect on the reader is also literary. The story does not primarily require our minds to grasp an idea but instead gets us to respond with our imagination and emotions to a real-life experience. It puts us on the scene and makes us participants in the action. It gets us involved with characters about whose destiny we are made to care. Literature, in short, is *affective,* not cool and detached. This, of course, made it such an effective teaching medium for Jesus, whose parables often drew his listeners innocently into the story and then turned the tables on them after it was too late to evade the issue at hand.

Reader
Involvement

What makes the parable of the good Samaritan a work of literature? Everything about it: its experiential approach to truth, its sensory concreteness, its narrative genre, its carefully crafted construction, and its total involvement of the reader— intellectually, emotionally, imaginatively.

SUMMARY

As Exhibit B, we consider the world's greatest poem, Psalm 23 (RSV):

Psalm 23 as a
Literary Work

The Lord is my shepherd, I shall not want;
  he makes me lie down in green pastures.
He leads me beside still waters;
  he restores my soul.
He leads me in paths of righteousness [right
    paths]
  for his name's sake.
Even though I walk through the valley of the
    shadow of death,
  I fear no evil;
for thou art with me;
  thy rod and thy staff,
  they comfort me.
Thou preparest a table before me
  in the presence of my enemies;

---

[3]Robert C. Tannehill, "Critical Discussion," *Semeia* 2 (1974): 115.

> thou anointest my head with oil,
>   my cup overflows.
> Surely goodness and mercy shall follow me
>   all the days of my life;
> and I shall dwell in the house of the Lord
>   for ever.

The Genre of Poetry

What indicates that this is literary writing? We can tell at a glance that this is poetry, another distinctly literary genre. The recurring unit is the poetic line, not the sentence. Furthermore, nearly every line follows the same grammatical pattern (God is identified as the actor, and then an action is ascribed to him), and many of the sentences fall into a pattern of pairs in which the second repeats the thought of the first in different words. In short, Psalm 23 is written in a verse form known as parallelism. It possesses a memorable, aphoristic quality that ordinary discourse lacks.

Unity and Shapeliness

There is equal artistry in the unity and shapeliness of the poem as a whole. The poem begins by announcing the theme and the controlling metaphor (the sheep-shepherd relationship). It then proceeds to a catalog of the shepherd's acts on behalf of his sheep, from the noontime resting in the shade to the activities performed in the sheepfold at the end of the day. And the poem ends with a forward-pointing note of finality. Psalm 23 has a self-contained, carefully crafted quality that we associate with art.

Literary Concreteness

Turning from the form to the content, we again sense how literary this text is. We see once more the literary impulse to be concrete instead of abstract. Psalm 23 takes God's providence as its subject. But the psalmist does not use the word *providence* and does not give us a theological definition of the concept. To drive this point home, we might contrast the literary approach of Psalm 23 with the theological definition of providence in the Westminster Confession of Faith:

> God the Creator of all things doth uphold, direct, dispose, and govern all creatures, actions, and things, from the greatest even to the least, by His most wise and holy providence. . . .

The approach of Psalm 23 is the opposite. It turns the idea of God's providence into a metaphor in which God is pictured as a shepherd in the daily routine of caring for his sheep. The literary approach of Psalm 23 is indirect: first we must picture what the shepherd does for his sheep, and then we must transfer that picture to the human level. Instead of using abstract, theological terminology, Psalm 23 consistently keeps us in a world of concrete images: green pastures, water, pathways, rod and staff, table, oil, cup, and sheepfold (metaphorically called a house).

How does literature work? Psalm 23 again shows us. Literature is concrete and experiential. It uses tangible images to convey the very quality of lived experience. It appeals to our imagination (image-making capacity). It conveys more meanings than ordinary expository language does—it would take several pages of expository prose to paraphrase all the meanings Psalm 23 compresses into nineteen lines. Psalm 23 is more concentrated, more consistently concrete, more obviously artistic, more eloquent and beautiful, than ordinary prose discourse.

The Differentia of Literature

The parable of the good Samaritan and Psalm 23 are typical of the kind of literary writing we keep running into as we read through the Bible. From these two examples I wish to branch out into a more systematic anatomy of the principles that underlie a literary approach to the Bible.

LITERATURE: THE VOICE OF HUMAN EXPERIENCE

It is a commonplace that the subject of literature is human experience—not abstract ideas or propositions, but experience. The knowledge or truth that literature gives us is an awareness of reality or truth as it is actually experienced.

The Subject of Literature: Human Experience

Literature, in other words, *shows* human experience instead of *telling about* it. It is incarnational. It enacts rather than states. Instead of giving us abstract propositions about virtue or vice, for example, literature presents stories of good or evil characters in action. The tendency of literature is to embody human experience, not to formulate ideas in intellectual propositions.

The Difference Between Literary and Expository Writing

We can profitably contrast the literary and the expository, or documentary, use of language. Expository ("explanatory") writing seeks to tell us, as objectively and clearly as possible, facts and information about a subject. Literature, by contrast, appeals to our imagination. Literature aims to recreate an experience or situation in sufficient detail and concreteness to enable the reader to relive it.

The Bible contains an abundance of both expository and literary writing. One is not inherently better or more effective than the other, and we obviously need both types of writing to do justice to all sides of life and truth. The commandment "you shall not kill" is expository in its approach to moral truth. The story of Cain and Abel (Gen. 4:1–16) embodies the same truth in the distinctly literary form of a story (a story that implies but nowhere states that it is sin to murder someone). When asked to define "neighbor," Jesus avoided expository discourse and instead told a parable.

Because literature aims to recreate a whole experience, there is a certain irreducible quality to it. We may be able to deduce ideas from a story or a poem, but those propositions are never an adequate substitute for the embodied vision that the literary work itself conveys. The whole story or the whole poem is the meaning because the truth that literature communicates is a living through of an experience. If the direct statement of an idea conveyed all that a story or poem does, the story or poem would be superfluous. But the stories and poems of the Bible are emphatically not superfluous.

The Need to Respect the Bible's Experiential Quality

What does it mean to approach the Bible as literature? It means first of all to be sensitive to the experiential side of the Bible. It means to resist the tendency to turn every biblical passage into a theological proposition, as though this is what the passage exists for. The one thing that the Bible is *not*, may I repeat, is a theological outline with proof texts.

THE CONCRETENESS OF LITERATURE

The chief means by which literature communicates the very quality of human experience is concreteness. In literature we constantly encounter the sights and sounds and vividness of real life. This is most easily seen in the poetry of the Bible. For the biblical poets, nothing remains wholly abstract. Longing for God becomes as tangible as thirst "in a dry and weary land where there is no water" (Ps. 63:1). Slander is pictured as weapon-toting ambushers "who sharpen their tongues like swords/and aim their words like deadly arrows" (Ps. 64:3). Pride becomes a necklace and violence a garment (Ps. 73:6).

Concreteness
in Biblical
Poetry

The impulse toward concreteness is no less prominent in the stories of the Bible. Even to express truth in the form of people doing things in specific settings is to choose a concrete medium rather than the abstract form of expository writing. It is easy to deduce a dozen ideas from the Bible's story of origins (Gen. 1–3) and to state these ideas as propositions, but the account itself almost totally avoids stating the truth about God and creation abstractly. It embodies everything in the concrete form of characters performing actions and saying things that we overhear.

The
Concreteness
of Biblical
Stories

Biblical stories exist on a continuum from a bare outline of what happened to a full account of how it happened. The more fully and concretely the story is told, the more literary we should consider it to be, and the stories of the Bible usually lean in the direction of literary concreteness. Consider a random passage from the Book of Acts (3:1–5):

> One day Peter and John were going up to the temple at the time of prayer—at three in the afternoon. Now a man crippled from birth was being carried to the temple gate called Beautiful, where he was put every day to beg from those going into the temple courts. When he saw Peter and John about to enter, he asked them for money. Peter looked straight at him, as did John. Then Peter said, "Look at us!" So the man gave them his attention, expecting to get something from them. . . .

A television camera could not have captured the event more vividly than this. If the writer's purpose were to state only *what* happened, there is a lot of excess baggage in the passage. But given the literary criterion of concreteness and vividness, the emphasis on *how* it happened is exactly what we should expect.

The Prominence of Dialogue in the Bible

We might also note in passing that one of the most distinctive traits of biblical writing, especially biblical stories, is the prevalence of direct speech and dialogue. Biblical storytellers are always busy quoting what characters said and giving us snatches of dialogue instead of indirect summaries of conversations. This, too, is part of the Bible's literary vividness. What could be more actual and immediate than the very words a character used?

Concreteness in New Testament Epistles

The impulse toward concrete vividness is not limited to the poetry and stories of the Bible. We find it in the Epistles, for example, mingled with the predominantly theological mode:

> Endure hardship with us as a good soldier of Christ Jesus. . . . An athlete . . . does not receive the victor's crown unless he competes according to the rules. The hard-working farmer should be the first to receive a share of the crops (2 Tim. 2:3, 5–6).

Even the letter as a form is more experiential and literary, less systematic and expository, than an essay or sermon.

SUMMARY

At the level of content, biblical literature is characterized by experiential concreteness. It is filled with the settings and sensations and actions of everyday life. It incarnates ideas in the form of poetic images, stories of characters in action, and living situations in which readers can imaginatively participate. It appeals to the understanding through the imagination.

The Need to Be Imaginative Readers

What is the practical result of this concreteness? It means that we should read the Bible with our imaginations (image-making capacity) as well as with our reason. If we are to read the Bible as literature, we must be active in recreating the experiences and sensations and events it portrays. We must be sensitive to the physical and experiential qualities of a passage and avoid reducing every passage in the Bible to a set of abstract themes. If we have "antennae" only for theological concepts or historical facts, we will miss much of what the Bible communicates and will distort the kind of book it is.

The Importance of Images

The Bible appeals to our imagination and emotions as well as to our reason and intellect. It conveys more than abstract ideas because its aim is to express the whole of *reality*. The Bible recognizes that a person's world view consists of images and symbols as well as ideas and propositions. A noted theologian has said that

> we are far more image-making and image-using creatures than we usually think ourselves to be and . . . are guided and formed by images in our minds. . . . Man . . . is a being who grasps and shapes reality . . . with the aid of great images, metaphors, and analogies.[4]

There is no better illustration of this than the Bible, an authoritative religious book that conveys the truth about reality by means of stories and characters and images and lifelike situations far oftener than by theological abstraction.

Truthfulness to Life and Reality

All of this affects how we should read the Bible. Reading the Bible as literature includes reading it for its ideas and implied assertions and themes, but it includes more than this. Literature conveys a sense of life—a sense of how the writer thinks and feels about what really exists, what is right and wrong, what is valuable and worthless. Literature can be *true to reality and human experience* as well as being the embodiment of a true proposition. Literature is true whenever we can say about its portrayal of life, "This is the way life is."

Reading the Bible to Absorb a Sense of Life

Reading biblical literature does not have to result in the intellectual grasp of an idea. We also read it to absorb or experience a sense of the way things truly are. In the parable of the good Samaritan, Jesus did not have to add a definition of "neighbor"; the meaning of the parable is complete if we *recognize* and *experience* the neighborly behavior

---

[4]H. Richard Niebuhr, *The Responsible Self* (New York: Harper and Row, 1963), 151–52, 161.

of the Samaritan. This has big implications for what might be called the devotional reading of the Bible. The stories and poems of the Bible achieve their devotional purpose whenever they reinforce a reader's general sense of the reality of God, or produce an awareness of what is moral and immoral, or influence a person's estimate of what is valuable and worthless. We are affected by more than ideas when we read literature, though, of course, ideas are part of the total experience. We read literature not primarily to acquire information but to contemplate experience and reality as a way of understanding them better. One of the rewards of reading literature, including the Bible, is that our own experiences and beliefs are given shape and expression.

Traditional approaches to the Bible lean heavily toward the conceptual and doctrinal. We have erroneously operated on the premise that a person's world view consists solely of abstract ideas— but it also includes stories and images. A literary approach to the Bible can go a long way toward respecting the other half of a person's world view—and the other side of the brain, to use contemporary psychological theory. The Bible is more than a book into which we reach for proof texts. What would happen if, instead of tracing ideas through the Bible, we traced a single image, such as light or food or garment or rock? We would have covered an amazing range of biblical doctrine, in a manner completely in keeping with the kind of book the Bible is.

LITERATURE REQUIRES INTERPRETATION

The Need to Interpret

From what I have already said it is easy to see why literature requires more of a reader than straightforward expository writing. Literature always calls for interpretation. It expresses its meanings by a certain indirection. The statement that "our neighbor is anyone whom we encounter in need of our help" is direct and requires no interpretation. By comparison, Jesus' parable of the good

Samaritan requires a reader to determine what the details in the story add up to.

The more concrete or complex a story is, the more open it becomes to interpretation. The story of David in the Old Testament illustrates this. What does the story of David communicate about God, people, and society? There is, of course, no single answer, nor is it always easy to determine exactly what truth is communicated by this or that episode in the story. It is no wonder that the story of David has elicited so many interpretations.[5]

Interpreting Stories

Biblical poetry also requires interpretation on the part of the reader. Consider, for example, the most important of all figures of speech: metaphor and simile. These figures of speech compare one thing to another: "He is like a tree planted by streams of water" (Ps. 1:3). Exactly *how* is the godly person like a tree? How many of the suggested points of comparison are valid? These are questions of interpretation that metaphor and simile always place before a reader.

Interpreting Poetry

If the need to interpret literature and the unavoidable differences in interpretation from one reader to another strike us as a risk, we should also note the advantages of literature as a medium. They include memorability, ability to capture a reader's attention, affective power, and ability to do justice to the complexity and multiplicity of human life as we actually experience it.

Some Advantages of the Literary Approach

THE ARTISTRY OF LITERATURE

Literature is an interpretive presentation of human experience. But it is more than that. It is also an art form, characterized by beauty, craftsmanship, and technique. Not merely *what* is said, but the *how* of a piece of writing is always important in literature.

The elements of artistic form that all types of literature (in fact, all art forms) share include pattern or design, theme or central focus, organic unity (also called unity in variety, or theme and

The Elements of Artistic Form

---

[5]For an overview, see *The David Myth in Western Literature*, ed. Raymond-Jean Frontain and Jan Wojcik (West Lafayette: Purdue University Press, 1980).

variation), coherence, balance, contrast, symmetry, repetition or recurrence, variation, and unified progression. In stories these ingredients will take one form, in poems another, as subsequent chapters in this book will show. But whatever the genre (literary type), the sheer abundance of literary technique and artistry that we find in many parts of the Bible make it a literary masterpiece that we can enjoy for its beauty as well read for its truth. What the writer of Ecclesiastes said about his own theory of composition applies equally to most biblical writers: he labored, he tells us, to arrange his material "with great care," and to "find pleasing words" or "words of delight" (Eccl. 12:9–10, RSV).

The Purposes of Artistry

What functions are served by this type of artistry? And why is it important to be aware of this dimension of the Bible? Artistic form serves the purpose of intensifying the impact of what is said, but also the purposes of pleasure, delight, and enjoyment. Artistry satisfies the human urge for beauty and craftsmanship. If a person set out to spend some time every day reading in the so-called sacred books of the world, I can predict which one most people would grow least tired of reading. Literary analysis is capable of showing why the Bible is an interesting book rather than a dull book to read. A famous detractor of biblical religion called the Bible "unquestionably the most beautiful book in the world."[6]

Reading with Artistic Sensitivity

What does the artistry of the Bible require of the reader? We need to be prepared to identify and enjoy the elements of literary form we find. A literary approach is sensitive to the artistic beauty of the Bible. It sees value in the craftsmanship of biblical writers. It relishes the stories and poems of the Bible as products of verbal and imaginative skill. That the Bible possesses such artistry is indisputable; the elements of artistic form and beauty I have mentioned are manifestly there. The only question is whether as readers we are prepared to recognize and enjoy the artistry. The artistic excellence of the Bible is not extraneous to its total effect. It is one of the glories of the Bible.

---

[6]H. L. Mencken, *Treatise on the Gods*, 2nd ed. (New York: Knopf, 1946), 286.

LITERARY GENRES

The commonest way of defining literature is by its genres, or literary types. Through the centuries, people have agreed that certain genres (such as story, poetry, and drama) are literary in nature. Other genres, such as historical chronicles, theological treatises, and genealogies, are expository (informational) in nature. Still others fall into one or the other category, depending on how the writer handles them. Letters, sermons, and orations, for example, can move in the direction of literature if they display the elements of literature discussed in this chapter.

Each literary genre has its distinctive features. Each has its own "rules" or procedures. This, in turn, affects how we read and interpret a work of literature. As readers we need to come to a given text with the right expectations. If we do, we will see more than we otherwise would, and we will avoid misreadings. If we know that stories are built around a central conflict leading to final resolution, we are in a position to see something that the writer has built into the story. Literary genre is nothing less than a "norm or expectation to guide the reader in his encounter with the text."[7] An awareness of genre will program our reading of a work, giving it a familiar shape and arranging the details into an identifiable pattern.

Knowing how a given genre works can spare us from misinterpretations. For example, exaggeration in a story that purports to be factual history is a form of untruth, while that same type of exaggeration in lyric poetry is called hyperbole and is a standard way of expressing emotional truth. The reliability of documentary history depends partly on the writer's inclusion of all the relevant historical material, but as interpreters we realize that literary narrative is much more selective and interpretive, incorporating material only to highlight the specific perspective a storyteller wishes to give to a character or event.

How important is the notion of genre to literature

Literary and Expository Genres

The Importance of Genres

---

[7]Jonathan Culler, *Structuralist Poetics* (Ithaca: Cornell University Press, 1975), 136.

and the Bible? Two biblical scholars answer that question at the beginning of a book on biblical interpretation:

> . . . the basic concern of this book is with the understanding of the different types of literature (the *genres*) that make up the Bible. Although we do speak to other issues, this generic approach has controlled all that has been done.[8]

A literary approach to the Bible agrees with this emphasis on literary genres, though it does not find the list of genres discussed by biblical scholars to be wholly adequate, nor is it totally satisfied with the scholars' descriptions of literary genres.

The Literary Genres of the Bible

The Bible is a mixture of genres, some literary, some expository, some mixed. The major *literary* genres are narrative or story, poetry (especially lyric poetry), proverb, and visionary writing (including prophecy and apocalypse). Historical writing in the Bible frequently moves in the direction of literary narrative by virtue of its experiential concreteness or the principles of pattern and design that permeate such writing. The epistles of the New Testament frequently become literary because their style is either poetic or artistic or both, and biblical satire usually employs a literary vehicle to communicate its attacks.

The Bible also has its share of genres that are either unique or decidedly hybrid, but these are sufficiently similar to familiar literary genres to yield their meanings if approached with literary tools. Biblical prophecy, for example, requires an ability to interpret poetry and satire. Biblical apocalypse is not a typical story, nor is it ordinary poetry, yet narrative and poetry are exactly the right categories with which to approach the Book of Revelation.

LITERATURE AS A SPECIAL USE OF LANGUAGE

Literary Language

Literature uses special resources of language in a way that people through the centuries have agreed to call literary. This quality cuts across literary

[8]Gordon D. Fee and Douglas Stuart, *How to Read the Bible for All Its Worth* (Grand Rapids: Zondervan, 1982), 11.

genres and, in fact, appears in texts that we would not consider to be primarily literary.

Literature exploits, for example, such devices of language as metaphor, simile, allusion, pun, paradox, and irony. Of course, these resources of language are the very essence of poetry, but the important thing about the Bible is that they appear everywhere, not just in the poetry. This is why, incidentally, a literary approach is necessary *throughout* the Bible and not just in the predominantly literary parts.

The story of Cain's murder of Abel (Gen. 4:1–16) illustrates how the stories of the Bible can use figurative language that we recognize as distinctly literary. When Cain becomes angry at his brother, God warns him that "sin is crouching at your door" (v. 7). This statement is an example of personification in which an abstract moral quality is figuratively treated as a person or animal. Biblical scholars disagree on whether sin is pictured here as "couching" or "crouching" at the door, but in either case we have to interpret the statement figuratively: sin is either a monster waiting to pounce on Cain if he does not get control of his anger, or it is a monster that, through long acquaintance, has become a familiar part of the household.

Literary Language in Biblical Stories

Later in the same story God tells Cain, "Your brother's blood cries out to me from the ground. . .which opened its mouth to receive your brother's blood from your hand" (vv. 10–11). This, too, is figurative and an obvious deviation from normal language. It shows that even in nonpoetic parts of the Bible the writers use literary and poetic resources of language. As readers we need to identify and interpret figurative language throughout the Bible. Indeed, there is *no* book of the Bible that is not partly literary.

This is true even of the most explicitly theological parts of the New Testament Epistles. Consider the following specimen:

Literary Language in Epistles

> Consequently, you are no longer foreigners and aliens, but fellow citizens with God's people and members of God's household, built on the foundation of the apostles and prophets, with Christ Jesus

himself as the chief cornerstone. In him the whole
building is joined together and rises to become a
holy temple in the Lord (Eph. 2:19–21).

The passage is thoroughly theological, but the
language is poetic. Almost everything is expressed
through metaphors: an unbeliever is an exile, a
believer is a citizen and family member, Christians
are a church building, and so on. It is hard to find a
page in the Bible that does not make at least some
use of the resources of language that are distinctly
literary.

Rhetorical Patterns in the Bible

Not only individual words and images but also
larger rhetorical patterns are a pervasive literary
presence in the Bible. Examples include parallelism
(two or more consecutive clauses arranged in
similar grammatical form), rhetorical questions,
question-and-answer constructions, imaginary dialogues, the aphoristic conciseness of a proverb,
and any highly patterned arrangement of clauses or
phrases (such as the intricate system of threes in
1 Cor. 13). A biblical scholar has analyzed the
presence of "tensive language," or "forceful and
imaginative language," in the New Testament; he
shows how such language uses rhetorical devices
to break through the clichés of ordinary language
and to reveal truth with power.[9] Such literary
resources pervade the entire Bible, even the sections that are not predominantly literary.

MEANING THROUGH FORM

The Primacy of Form in the Bible

A literary approach to the Bible is preoccupied
with literary *form*, and that for a very good reason.
In any written discourse, meaning is communicated
through form. The concept of "form" should be
construed very broadly in this context: it includes
anything that touches upon *how* a writer has
expressed his content. Everything that gets communicated does so through form, beginning with
language itself.

[9]Robert C. Tannehill, *The Sword of His Mouth: Forceful
and Imaginative Language in Synoptic Sayings* (Philadelphia: Fortress, 1975).

While this is true for all forms of writing, it is especially crucial for literature. Literature has its own forms and techniques, and these tend to be more complex and subtle and indirect than those of ordinary discourse. Stories, for example, communicate their meaning through character, setting, and action. The result is that before we can understand what a story says we must first interact with the form, that is, the characters, settings, and events. Poetry conveys its meanings through figurative language and concrete images. It is therefore impossible to determine what a poem says without first encountering the form (metaphor, simile, image, etc.).

Literature Uses Unique Forms to Communicate Meaning

The literary critic's preoccupation with the *how* of biblical writing is not frivolous. It is evidence of an artistic delight in verbal beauty and craftsmanship, but it is also part of an attempt to understand *what* the Bible says. In a literary text it is impossible to separate what is said from how it is said, content from form.

Form and Content Are Inseparable

LOOKING FOR LITERARY WHOLES

The most basic of all artistic principles is unity. The literary approach to the Bible accordingly looks for literary patterns and wholeness of effect. Richard G. Moulton, pioneer of the literary approach to the Bible, wrote, "No principle of literary study is more important than that of grasping clearly a literary work as a single whole."[10] This literary preoccupation with the overall unity and pattern of biblical works stands in contrast to traditional approaches. Austin Farrar, a biblical scholar with excellent literary intuitions, criticizes his own discipline on precisely this point:

The Importance of Unity

> Form-criticism [as practiced by biblical scholars] is rather misleadingly so called, because the name suggests an attempt to appreciate the form of a complete literary unit, say St Mark's Gospel. Whereas what form-criticism studies is the form of the small constituent parts of the Gospels; anecdotal paragraphs, for example, or even such small

---

[10]*The Modern Reader's Bible* (New York: Macmillan, 1895), 1719.

details as apparently self-contained gnomic sentences. . . . In the literary realm, . . . the pattern of the whole comes first.[11]

Traditional and Literary Approaches Contrasted

The tendency of biblical scholars to divide a biblical text into pieces has taken two forms. One is the penchant of liberal scholars for undertaking textual "excavations" in an attempt to determine the various strata in the development of a text from its original form to its final written form. The other is the practice of conservative scholars to organize the Bible into a theological outline and then treat various verses or passages as proof texts. Both procedures end up dividing a text into fragments, as does the verse-by-verse commentary that is such a staple of biblical scholarship. The literary approach to the Bible, by contrast, accepts the biblical text in its final form as the focus of study. It assumes unity in a text. The resultant ability to see the overall pattern of a story or poem is one of the greatest gifts that a literary approach confers.

SUMMARY

The Bible demands a literary approach because its writing is literary in nature. The Bible is an experiential book that conveys the concrete reality of human life. It is filled with evidences of literary artistry and beauty, much of it in the form of literary genres. It also makes continuous use of resources of language that we can regard as literary. A literary approach pays close attention to all of these elements of literary form, because it is through them that the Bible communicates its message.

The literary approach to the Bible is becoming increasingly popular among both biblical and literary scholars. Traditional approaches to the Bible seem to have reached something of an impasse.[12]

---

[11]*A Study in St Mark* (London: Dacre, 1951), 21–22.

[12]It is hard to pick up a scholarly religious journal these days without catching hints of a discipline in transition. For a concentrated initiation into the current state of the discipline, the best source is the essays collected in *Orientation by Disorientation: Studies in Literary Criticism and Biblical Literary Criticism,* ed. Richard A. Spencer (Pittsburgh: Pickwick, 1980).

Given the literary nature of the Bible, it is not surprising that biblical scholars are turning to the methods of literary criticism as a way of understanding and discussing the Bible. "I would hope," writes one of them, "that the new approaches will remain as receptive to literary analysis as they are at the present time. . . . It may well be—and I regard this as highly desirable—that biblical literary criticism will be deparochialized and reintegrated with non-religious literary criticism in the future."[13] "Literary criticism is not . . . just the latest faddish approach," writes another; "it represents a significant shift in perspective. . . ."[14] My purpose in the pages that follow is to make the methods of literary criticism more accessible to anyone who reads and studies the Bible.

Further Reading

In keeping with the focus of the opening chapter, the sources that I list here deal in a *theoretical* way with what it means to approach the Bible as literature. I must sound a note of warning in regard to sources that are sometimes included in lists such as this. *Not everything that claims to be a literary approach to the Bible actually is;* in fact, most of what has been written to date has not been a genuinely literary approach.

An immense quantity of literary criticism of the Bible has been collected in companion volumes to be published as part of Frederick Ungar's *Library of Literary Criticism* series; the editors are Alex Preminger and Edward L. Greenstein for the Old Testament and Leland Ryken for the New Testament. The sources listed in another reference book, J. H. Gottcent's *The Bible as Literature: A Selective Bibliography* (Boston: G. K. Hall, 1979), are a mixed group, more indicative of the methods of biblical scholarship than of literary criticism.

Examples of biblical scholars whose theory of biblical analysis is essentially literary include Wil-

[13]William G. Doty, *Letters in Primitive Christianity* (Philadelphia: Fortress, 1973), 79, 81.
[14]Robert M. Fowler, "Using Literary Criticism on the Gospels," *Christian Century*, 26 May 1982, 627.

liam A. Beardslee, *Literary Criticism of the New Testament* (Philadelphia: Fortress, 1970); Amos N. Wilder, *Early Christian Rhetoric: The Language of the Gospel* (Cambridge: Harvard University Press, 1971), and *Jesus' Parables and the War of Myths: Essays on Imagination in the Scripture*, ed. James Breech (Philadelphia: Fortress, 1982); Robert C. Tannehill, *The Sword of His Mouth: Forceful and Imaginative Language in Synoptic Sayings* (Philadelphia: Fortress, 1975); James A. Fischer, *How to Read the Bible* (Englewood Cliffs: Prentice-Hall, 1981), pp. 30–45; J. P. Fokkelman, *Narrative Art and Poetry in the Books of Samuel*, vol. 1 (Assen, The Netherlands: Van Gorcum, 1981), especially pp. 1–18; Norman R. Petersen, "Literary Criticism in Biblical Studies," in *Orientation by Disorientation*, ed. Richard A. Spencer (Pittsburgh: Pickwick, 1980), pp. 25–50.

Literary scholars who have applied their methods to the Bible include Roland M. Frye, "A Literary Perspective for the Criticism of the Gospels," in *Jesus and Man's Hope, II*, ed. Donald G. Miller and Dikran Y. Hadidian (Pittsburgh: Pittsburgh Theological Seminary, 1971), pp. 193–221; and also "The Synoptic Problems and Analogies in Other Literatures," in *The Relationships among the Gospels: An Interdisciplinary Dialogue*, ed. William O. Walker, Jr. (San Antonio: Trinity University Press, 1978), pp. 261–302; Leland Ryken, *The Literature of the Bible* (Grand Rapids: Zondervan, 1974); selected contributors to *Literary Interpretations of Biblical Narratives*, vols 1, 2, ed. Kenneth R. R. Gros Louis (Nashville: Abingdon, 1974 and 1982); Robert Alter, *The Art of Biblical Narrative* (New York: Basic Books, 1981); Northrop Frye, *The Great Code: The Bible and Literature* (New York: Harcourt Brace Jovanovich, 1982).

Most promising of all is the model represented by a literary critic and a biblical scholar who combined their respective areas of expertise: David Rhoads and Donald Michie, *Mark as Story* (Philadelphia: Fortress, 1982).

Chapter Two

The Stories of
the Bible

GOD MADE PEOPLE BECAUSE HE LOVES STORIES. So claims
a rabbinic saying. Henry R. Luce, founder of *Time
Magazine*, quipped, "*Time* didn't start this emphasis on stories about people; the Bible did."

Narrative is the dominant form in the Bible. Its
prominence is well captured in Amos Wilder's oft-
quoted statement that "the narrative mode is
uniquely important in Christianity."[1] What this
means to readers of the Bible is that the more they
know about how stories work, the more they will
enjoy and understand vast portions of the Bible.

The stories of the Bible vary widely in regard to
the fullness with which they are told. Some are
entries in a historical chronicle; they obey the
documentary impulse to tell what happened, avoiding the literary impulse to present in detail *how* it
happened.

At the other end of the continuum we find full-
fledged stories like those of David and Job. These
obey the literary impulse to *present* an event rather
than simply tell about it. They are full, circumstan-
tial, and embellished with detail, and they allow the
reader to recreate the story in his or her imagination.

Not every sequence of events in the Bible is a
story in the literary sense of that term. Given the
continuum that ranges from a bare summary of

**The
Prominence of
Stories in the
Bible**

**Historical
Documentation
Versus Literary
Narrative**

---

[1] *Early Christian Rhetoric: The Language of the Gospel*
(Cambridge: Harvard University Press, 1971), 56.

33

events to a full account of how the events occurred, the closer a story is to the detailed end of the spectrum, the more justified we are in approaching it with the interpretive tools outlined in this chapter.

Stories as an Invitation to Share an Experience

Whenever a biblical storyteller goes beyond the documentary impulse to record what happened and proceeds to describe how it happened, he thereby signals that he wishes us, the readers, to share an *experience,* perhaps a prolonged experience, with one or more characters. The phenomenon known as identifying with characters in a story involves a reader's going through the action with a specific character.

Readers as Participants and Spectators

The implication of this experiential dimension of stories is that as readers we must be active, either as participants or as spectators. The power of story as a literary form is its uncanny ability to involve us in what is happening. Storytellers put us on the scene and in the middle of an action. They pluck us out of our own time and place and put us into another time and place. As Norman Perrin puts it, "The natural function of narrative is to help the reader hear the voices, take part in the action, get involved in the plot."[2] The more vividly storytellers portray the action and characters and settings, the more compelling is their sway over our attention, as the biblical storytellers knew so well.

The Need to Be an Active Reader

To read stories well, then, we need to be active—in visualizing, in imagining scenes, in entering into the spirit of events, in identifying with characters. One sure way to impoverish our experience of a biblical story is to remain outside of the action, as though we were simply being told a series of facts. Personal involvement, achieved by an active use of the imagination, is the first requirement for reading biblical narrative. The stories of the Bible demand the answering imagination of the reader for their effect.

Rule number one for reading the stories of the Bible is simply this: *look upon biblical stories as an invitation to share an experience, as vividly and*

[2] *The New Testament: An Introduction* (New York: Harcourt Brace Jovanovich, 1974), 165.

concretely as possible, with the characters in the story.

Stories are always built out of three basic ingredients: setting, characters, and plot (action). Reading a story involves paying attention to the interaction of these three elements.

The Basic Ingredients

The setting of a story is simultaneously physical, temporal, and cultural. The physical scenes that storytellers build into their stories serve several functions. They are usually a necessary background for understanding the action that occurs within them. They are of course an important part of the concrete vividness by which storytellers enable their readers to enter fully into the experience of a story. They may be an important part of the identity of a character (as when Abraham, the nomad and domestic hero, is repeatedly linked with rural landscapes and tents).

The Functions of Settings

Physical settings can also establish the atmosphere or tone of a story. The atmosphere of danger from which Peter is delivered in Acts 12 is effectively established by scenic details of prison, guards, chains, and iron gates. The hostility of Joseph's brothers (Gen. 37) is actively abetted by the details of setting that the storyteller chose to record—the remoteness of the region, such features of landscape as open pits, and the nearness of the route traveled by trading caravans.

Physical Settings Build Atmosphere

In addition to their literal meaning, physical settings often assume a thematic or symbolic meaning in biblical stories. The idealized love story of Ruth and Boaz is reinforced by the rural (pastoral) imagery of growing crops and harvests. Spiritual revelations often occur on mountains (e.g., Moses' meeting with God on Mount Sinai, Elijah's encounter with the prophets of Baal on Mount Carmel, and Jesus' transfiguration on the Mount of Olives). The symbolic use of geography in the synoptic Gospels and Book of Acts is also well known: in the Gospels, Galilee is the place chosen by God to reveal his salvation and Jerusalem is the place of rejection; the Book of Acts opens in Jerusalem, seat of the Jewish religion that rejected the Gospel, and ends after a long travel

Symbolic Meanings of Settings

section in Rome, capital of the Gentile world to which the Gospel was sent.

Settings and Structural Unity

Another function of physical settings is to lend structural unity to a story. The episodic plot of the Exodus is unified in part by the continuous references to wilderness, water, fire, and rock. The story of Elijah is repeatedly linked with hills and mountains, the story of Jacob with rocks. Events in Genesis are joined by a common pastoral (rural) setting, and those in the books of Esther and Daniel by the continuous references to court life. The movement from Galilee to Jerusalem is an important structural principle in the synoptic Gospels, just as the transfer of action from Jerusalem to Rome in the Book of Acts gives shape to both the action and the theology of the story.

Temporal Settings

Stories have a temporal setting as well as a physical setting, and this, too, can be important to the overall impact of a story. It is important in the story of Esther that the events occurred during the Jewish exile in Persia, when the Jews were a vulnerable minority. The impact of the story of Jonah depends on our knowing that the action occurs at a time in history when Nineveh was the capital of the world-conquering Assyrians, known for their cruelty and terrorism.

Cultural Settings

The setting of a story includes, finally, a whole cultural climate—the set of beliefs, attitudes, and customs that prevail in the world of the story. Without the information biblical scholars have uncovered about ancient cultural practices, modern readers become prime candidates to misread the stories of the Bible. Did Jacob steal the birthright from Esau? Technically he bought it (and cleverly made the bargain binding by insisting that Esau swear an oath as he smelled the pottage), based on the practice among ancient Hurrians of transferring a birthright from one brother to another through negotiation and payment. The opening verse of Ruth, which tells us that "a man from Bethlehem in Judah, together with his wife and two sons, went to live for a while in the country of Moab," is a bland piece of factual data until we know something about the ancient hostility between Jew and Moabite. Once we know the cultural background, the statement explodes with hidden suspense, as if a contemporary novelist were to begin a story, "In 1946 a certain Jewish family went to Germany."[3]

Many readers ignore the settings in biblical stories, but to do so is to miss much of the meaning. Sometimes, it is true, setting functions as little more than a lead-in to a story (for example, "Jesus began to teach by the lake" in Mark 4:1). But whenever a storyteller begins to elaborate the setting, we can rest assured that it is there for a purpose, either to make the story come alive in our imagination or as a contribution to the meaning of the story. Many of the stories of the Bible devote so much attention to scenic details that these details are virtually stage directions in a play.

Rule two for reading the stories of the Bible is therefore this: *pay close attention to every detail of setting that a storyteller puts into a story, and if setting has an important role, analyze how it contributes to the story.*

The Importance of Paying Attention to a Story's Setting

The old debate whether character or plot is more important in a story is one that need not detain us. Character is what produces action; on the other hand, characters are known to us through their actions. The important thing is to be alert to the way in which character and plot work together to produce the total effect.

The Role of Character in Narrative

It is useful to be aware of the means by which a storyteller can portray a character. One is direct description. When a biblical storyteller informs us that "Joseph was well-built and handsome" (Gen. 39:6) or that Esther "was lovely in form and features" (Esth. 2:7), all we need to do is take the writer's word for it. No further interpretation is required from us. It is significant to note, though, that this type of direct description is very sparse in the stories of the Bible. Even in the Gospels it is the exception rather than the rule for the authors to clarify Jesus' motivation by telling us that he was angry or moved with compassion.

How Characters Are Portrayed: 1. Direct Description by the Storyteller

[3]This formulation comes from Samuel Sandmel, *The Enjoyment of Scripture* (London: Oxford University Press, 1972), 26.

**2. Other
Characters'
Responses**

A second way in which we know characters in a story is through other characters' responses to them. Our picture of Jesus in the Gospels is repeatedly determined by the way in which humble and oppressed people flock to him in admiration, while the people with religious and civil power hate him. The responses of a series of Persian kings to Daniel establish him firmly in our imagination as a person of distinguished ability and personal integrity, as does the fact that his personal enemies admit among themselves that "we will never find any basis for charges against this man Daniel unless it has something to do with the law of his God" (Dan. 6:5).

**3. A
Character's
Words and
Thoughts**

A third way to know a character is through the thoughts and words of that character. To sense that Abraham is a family man, Jacob a schemer, Ruth a gentle woman, and Jesus a person of compassion and authority as the occasion demanded, all we need to do is pay attention to their characteristic thought patterns and recorded speeches.

**4. Self-
Characterization**

To have persons in a story characterize themselves is also a way of revealing character to us. The great example is of course Jesus, when in the Gospels he repeatedly explains himself and his mission. But there are other notable examples of the same technique in biblical narrative: Job's repeated portrayal of himself as an innocent person, King Saul's admission that David is more righteous than he is (1 Sam. 24:17), or the autobiographical strand in many of Paul's speeches in Acts.

**5. Actions as a
Clue to
Character**

There are, indeed, numerous ways in which a character emerges from the pages of the Bible as a full-fledged person. Mainly, though, the characters are known to us by their actions. It is a commonplace that the stories of the Bible tend to be told in a very spare, unembellished style. We are told only the most important things, and this usually means that the writer concentrates on showing us a character in action. The alternating of Abraham between faith and expediency, the courage of Ruth, the moral perfection of Jesus—these character traits emerge mainly from the actions we observe the characters performing.

Whenever a storyteller decides to let a character's actions do the talking, he thereby places a burden of interpretation on the reader. Often we know exactly how to interpret an action because we can place it into the context of moral commands elsewhere in the Bible. When Cain murders Abel, when David commits adultery with Bathsheba, or when Ananias and Sapphira lie, we have no difficulty in judging their characters negatively on that point. Conversely, when Abraham exercises faith in God or shows generosity toward his nephew, or when Joseph resists sexual temptation, we do not need to take a Gallup poll before concluding that they are examples of moral virtue.

Characterization Involves a Reader's Interpretation

But there are many other places in the stories of the Bible where the assessment of what a character is like is open to alternative interpretations. Is the youthful Joseph's telling Jacob about his brothers' bad behavior an example of moral courage or ignominious self-serving? Why does Joseph manipulate his brothers before revealing himself to them? Did Esther compromise her religious principles when she fit in so well at the Persian court that she even managed to keep her Jewish identity a total secret? Many of the stories of the Bible raise interpretive questions like these, and we need only read around in the commentaries to see what a lack of consensus there is on some of them. Because biblical stories leave so much unstated, they are "fraught with background and mysterious," "greatly in need of interpretation," writes Erich Auerbach in his classic study of the plain style of biblical narrative.[4]

The practical result is that we must get maximum mileage out of the few details that are given regarding the characters in the brief, unembellished stories of the Bible. It also means that we are often left to choose somewhat tentatively from among alternative interpretations of character and action. "The Bible's highly laconic mode of narration," writes Robert Alter, captures "an abiding mystery in character as the biblical writers conceive it,

Paying Attention to Details

---

[4]*Mimesis: The Representation of Reality in Western Literature,* trans. Willard Trask (Princeton: Princeton University Press, 1953), ch. 1. A truly great essay.

which they embody in their typical methods of presentation."[5] In virtually all cases of ambiguous or uncertain characterization, the main point of the story is unaffected by disagreements on how to interpret a character's motivation or behavior at a given point in the story.

SUMMARY

Characters are an essential part of any biblical story. Therefore, the third rule for reading stories is, *use every relevant detail in a story to get to know the characters as fully as possible*.

A Definition of Plot

The plot of a story is the arrangement of the events. That arrangement is not random. A plot is a coherent sequence of interrelated events, with a beginning, middle, and end. It is, in other words, a *whole* or complete action.[6]

Conflict: The Heart of Plot

The essence of plot is a central conflict or set of conflicts moving toward a resolution. One of the very first things to pay attention to when reading a story is the conflicts that organize the story from the very beginning. They can be of several types.

Types of Plot Conflict: 1. Physical Conflict

Most stories involve some type of physical conflict. Throughout the Bible we read about characters struggling for survival against physical adversity and danger. In fact, the stories of the Bible are a nearly continuous series of either narrow escapes or calamities. This is not surprising, for conflict against physical forces has always been a staple in the stories of the world. Of course, the struggle for physical survival in biblical stories usually provides the occasion for some further (frequently spiritual) action. But if we are to read these narratives as stories, we must first of all respond to the literal situations, preferably as a child responds to stories of physical danger.

Such stories are among the best-known ones in the Bible. The struggle for physical survival is the background against which Abraham, Jacob, and

[5]*The Art of Biblical Narrative* (New York: Basic Books, 1981), 126, 184.

[6]Aristotle's *Poetics,* especially chs. 7–11, 17, and 23, has been rather definitive on the nature of plot through the centuries, and it continues to be the best starting point on the subject.

Joseph live out their lives in the stories of Genesis. The story of the Exodus is a never-ending series of shortages of food and water. As for that perennial favorite, the narrow escape, we find it repeatedly in the Bible—in the stories of Jacob and Elijah and David and Daniel, in the Gospels, in the Book of Acts. We should not minimize the element of physical conflict in the stories of the Bible; it is a major element in the stories, either as the thing that arouses our narrative interest or as the occasion for a religious theme (such as the providential emphasis that is so recurrent in biblical narrative).

Conflicts can also occur between characters. Many of the famous stories in the Bible are built around great character clashes: Cain and Abel, Jacob and Esau, Joseph and his brothers, the Israelites and their oppressors, Jonah and God, Elijah and Jezebel, Jesus and the Jewish leaders, Paul and the Jews. The best way of organizing a discussion of such stories is obviously around the development of the character conflict.

2. Character Conflicts

Still other plot conflicts are primarily moral or spiritual. They occur chiefly within a character. The story of Cain and Abel, despite the external violence, is ultimately a story of good in conflict with evil. So is the story of Jezebel's seizing of Naboth's vineyard. Job fights an inner battle to understand his suffering and to maintain his faith in God in the midst of that suffering. Jesus went through an agonizing inner struggle in the Garden of Gethsemane.

3. Moral or Spiritual Conflicts

Stories are always built around plot conflicts. These conflicts progress toward some type of resolution, and when the resolution occurs, closure comes quickly. Noting plot conflicts is one of the best ways to organize a story, either in the actual process of reading or when talking about the story.

SUMMARY

The fourth rule for reading stories is to *identify the exact nature of the plot conflicts in a story, noting how they develop and are finally resolved.*

Regardless of what else we might say about stories, the basic characteristic that determines whether they succeed or fail is the element of

Narrative Suspense

suspense, that is, the ability to arouse the reader's curiosity. The novelist E. M. Forster has described the matter very succinctly: as story, a narrative "can only have one merit: that of making the audience want to know what happens next. And conversely it can only have one fault: that of making the audience not want to know what happens next."[7] This applies also to stories in the Bible.

How Stories Awaken Our Curiosity

To engage our continuing interest, storytellers must make us want to know how a given situation will turn out. The means by which storytellers generate this kind of curiosity are multiple, but the most universal one is plot conflict that calls for progression and final resolution. Putting characters into situations of danger or testing is therefore a staple in storytelling. An alternative way of eliciting reader interest is portraying vivid or striking characters about whose destiny we are made to care. Again, in biblical stories encounters between humans and God, even when the encounters do not involve conflict, generate interest about how the meeting will turn out.

Analyzing How a Story Generates Interest

Two of the most productive questions I have learned to ask about a given story or episode within it are, "Exactly what accounts for the narrative interest that this story elicits from me?" and, "How does it make me a participant in the action?" These questions are a good entry into the specific details of a given text. We might note in passing that some stories make us wonder *what* the outcome will be, whereas with other stories we already know the outcome but are led to wonder *how* that outcome will be achieved. The classic example of the latter type is the story of Joseph, where the destined ending of the story (Joseph's triumph over his brothers) is announced at the beginning, but where we could not possibly guess from the opening situation how that ending could be achieved.

An additional rule for interacting with biblical stories is this: *in reading or discussing the stories*

---

[7]*Aspects of the Novel* (1927; reprint, Harmondsworth: Penguin, 1962), 35. This book contains an abundance of good narrative theory.

of the Bible, analyze exactly how the narrative generates interest, curiosity, or suspense.

Every story has a central character. This is simply one of the principles of selectivity and emphasis that storytellers impose on their material. The central character is called the protagonist of the story, and the forces arrayed against him or her are the antagonists.

The Presence of a Central Protagonist

Readers and interpreters of biblical stories would do much better with these stories than they often do if they followed a very simple rule: *pay attention to what happens to the protagonist in the story.* Stories are built around the protagonist. You can't go far wrong with a story if you simply go through the action as the observant traveling companion of the protagonist in the story.

There are several related points that are equally practical. It is helpful to view the protagonist of the story as someone who undertakes an experiment in living. This experiment in living is tested during the course of the action, and its final success or failure is a comment on the adequacy of the protagonist's morality or world view on which the experiment was based. Abraham's life, for example, is a venture in faith. Called by God and given nothing more tangible than some promises, Abraham packs up his belongings and follows God's call. He has momentary lapses of faith, but his experiment in living is ultimately vindicated. He is blessed by God and dies at peace with himself and the world.

The Protagonist's Experiment in Living

A protagonist's experiment in living might be weighed in the balance and found wanting. Once Saul has been propelled into the kingship of Israel, his experiment in leadership is to maintain his popularity with the people by doing what is expedient instead of obeying God. The tragic form into which the story is cast becomes a negative interpretation of Saul's experiment in living, showing that it failed.

Teaching by Negative Example

A related principle is that the protagonist of a story is intended to be representative or exemplary of a whole segment of humanity, and perhaps of the whole human race. That is in part why writers choose to tell a given story. In the words of the modern fiction writer Flannery O'Connor, "Any

The Protagonist as Our Representative

character . . . is supposed to carry a burden of meaning larger than himself.''[8] This universality is, in fact, one of the distinctive features of literature, as theorists from Aristotle on have noted. To test whether a story has this quality of being perpetually up-to-date is simple: if we can see our own experience in the events and characters of the story, the story has captured something universal about life. Every sermon based on a biblical narrative assumes that what happens to the characters in the story is somehow a model of the enduring human situation.

A Literary Approach Stresses the Universality of a Story

This shows the difference between a literary approach to the Bible and a historical approach. The task of the historian is to record what *happened;* the task of the literary storyteller is to tell us what *happens.* The two ways of recording events can be combined; in the Bible they *have* been combined, and biblical stories can therefore be approached as history as well as literature. The literary approach is one that explores the story as an experience with enduring relevance. We should perhaps note that this approach has more in common with preaching and ordinary Bible reading than the more historical interests of specialized biblical scholars.

The foregoing discussion of the protagonist in biblical stories yields an important principle for reading biblical narrative: *look upon the protagonist's experiment in living as a comment about a significant aspect of human life and values.*

Narrative Unity

Stories are unified wholes. In any well-told story there is a unifying framework within which everything in the story finds a place. Few things are as debilitating to a discussion of a biblical story than a failure to lay out the unifying pattern(s) of the story. In the absence of such a framework, the story remains a series of disjointed and isolated fragments. Three basic principles on which stories are built are unity, coherence, and emphasis. These are, perhaps, the *last* things we discover as we read through a story, since they are not fully evident until the story is finished. But the unity and

---

[8]*Mystery and Manners,* ed. Sally and Robert Fitzgerald (New York: Farrar, Strauss & Giroux, 1957), 167.

coherence of a story are virtually the *first* things we should mention when discussing a biblical story.

One of the first things to do with a story is to determine its precise boundaries. This involves deciding where the story begins and ends within the surrounding biblical text. Sometimes this delineation depends on a reader's or commentator's purpose at the moment. For example, it is quite possible to treat the story of Abraham's willingness to sacrifice Isaac (Gen. 22) as a self-contained story. But that same material becomes only an episode if we are discussing the story of Abraham as a whole.

Identifying Where a Story Begins and Ends

Determining the shape of a story entails not only fixing its boundaries but also dividing it into its scenes or episodes. A good study Bible has already done most of this work for the reader. It is important to attach accurate headings to each scene or episode, since these units become the major building blocks in constructing our conception of the overall movement of the story. Once we have determined the overall shape and individual episodes of a story, we can proceed to the further question of narrative unity.

Dividing a Story into Scenes or Episodes

Narrative unity can be of several types. Aristotle theorized that the unifying element in a story is a "unity of plot. . . , not as some persons think. . .unity of hero." This is generally true, but Aristotle underestimated the ability of a literary hero to impose a satisfactory unity on a story. Even in stories that have unity of plot, the presence of the protagonist throughout the action also lends unity to the story. When we recall the stories of Abraham, Jacob, Joseph, Ruth, Esther, and Jesus, our impressions of the stories organize themselves partly around the hero or heroine.

Unity of Hero

When a story is unified *only* by the presence of the hero, and not by a corresponding unity of action, its plot is called *episodic*. In such a story, the events succeed each other but do not form a cause–effect chain in which one event produces the next. The episodes in such a story can be rearranged or deleted without destroying the flow of the story. Such episodic plots are rare but not unknown in the Bible. The first six chapters of

Episodic Plots

Daniel are six separate ordeals, joined only by the fact that they all involve Daniel or his acquaintances. The story of David is even more episodic. The Gospels, despite the presence of unifying motifs and a general chronological movement, are basically episodic plots.

Unity of Action

In general, however, narrative unity implies that a story deals with *one* action. Out of the mass of events that constitute the life of a person, the storyteller selects a single action for the purpose of a given story. The story of Gideon, for example, is unified by more than the presence of the hero throughout the story; it is a single action— Gideon's conquest of the Midianites. The story of Jacob is built around the hero's struggle with his own character flaws and his family. The story of Joseph is unified by the hero's quest to fulfill the destiny announced at the very beginning of the story. Out of all the things the author might have written about Ruth, the storyteller selected details that contribute to the motif of Ruth's quest for a home in a foreign land.

Multiple Plots

Occasionally a story in the Bible is sufficiently complex to be called a multiple plot. But even in those cases the action is carefully controlled and shaped. Each thread of action, when isolated from the others, meets the test of being a single, self-contained action with a beginning, middle, and end. The story of Abraham is a good example. It consists of at least four interrelated but discernible actions: (1) the chronological shape of the hero's life from age seventy-five to his death; (2) the progressive revelation of the covenant that God repeatedly announces to Abraham; (3) the quest for a son and descendants and land; (4) the hero's struggle between faith and expediency. The plot is multiple, but it is not episodic, because each thread of action follows the principles of coherence and unity.

Cause-Effect Connections Among Events

Unity of plot implies not only that the writer has selected details to fit a single action—it also implies the principle of causal coherence among the events. A unified plot is not a mere succession or accumulation of events but a sequence of events that are linked by a chain of cause and effect. In a famous reformulation of Aristotle's theory that episodes in a story follow one another by "probable or necessary sequence," novelist E. M. Forster wrote that the mere sequence "the king died and then the queen died" does not constitute a plot. But the statement "the king died and then the queen died of grief" does contain a plot in kernel form.[9] For me, the most convenient test of whether a story has such causal coherence is to begin at the end of a story and march backward through the main events. (Others may prefer to start at the beginning and proceed to the end.) If, for each major episode, I can say that a given event happened *because of* the previous one, the story has causal coherence.

How important is it to engage in such plot analysis? There can be no doubt that the concentrated impact of a story depends heavily on the presence of causal coherence. Plots that are too loose or random make weak stories. Furthermore, a story will remain largely a series of fragments in the reader's mind unless he or she has some framework for recognizing the coherence among the episodes. Analyzing the cause–effect connections between events in a story is one good way to discern the coherence of a story.

How to Discern Coherence

Other ways of becoming aware of the coherence of stories may work just as well, such as simply being alert to how a character or situation changes or progresses or is reinforced as we move from one event to the next. In hero stories, for example, each episode turns out to be a variation on the theme of defining the hero, but close scrutiny usually reveals that with each successive episode we learn something new about the hero, and often the very order in which we learn those things is important.

To discern the unity of stories with multiple plots, it is useful to arrange the unifying patterns into a chart or diagram. In the story of Abraham, for example, we can isolate four main narrative concerns: (1) defining the hero; (2) progressive revelation of the covenant; (3) the quest for a son

Charting the Progress of a Story

---

[9]*Aspects of the Novel*, 93.

The Genesis Passage	12: 1–9	12: 10–20	13	14	15	16	17	18: 1–15	18: 16–23	19	20	21: 1–7	21: 8–21	21: 22–34	22	23	24	25
Defining the Hero	X	X	X	X	X	X	X	X	X	X	X	X	X	X	X	X	X	X
Progressive Revelation of the Covenant Promise	X		X		X	X	X	X							X			
Quest for a Son and Descendants	X		X		X	X	X	X				X			X			
Conflict Between Faith and Expediency: Faith	X		X		X										X		X	
Conflict Between Faith and Expediency: Expediency		X				X	X				X		X					

and descendants; (4) the conflict between faith and expediency. The diagram on page 48 allows us to see at a glance what motifs appear in the successive episodes.

Several things stand out. The only motif that is picked up in every episode is the emerging portrait of the hero, confirming that the literary family of the story is heroic narrative and demonstrating that unity of hero dominates the story. The diagram also shows that the storyteller had a good grasp of the narrative principle of variety; he avoided monotony by picking and choosing among the various narrative threads (never, however, leaving a given narrative concern untouched for too long). The chart suggests at a glance how interrelated the various levels of action are. It also shows that the hero's vacillation between faith and expediency persists nearly to the end of the story (being decisively resolved in Genesis 22, the episode of the sacrifice of Isaac). The completed diagram also confirms that Abraham's willingness to sacrifice his son is the climax of the whole story, since all the main actions converge at this late point in the story.

Mainly, though, the chart underscores the principle that we must recognize in every narrative, even one that has a single plot line: it is crucial to see how a given episode relates to the overriding framework(s) of the story. Individual episodes in a story are not self-contained but exist in the context of the whole story. As Aristotle said regarding the individual episodes of a story, "We must see that they are relevant to the action." With or without the use of a diagram, relating episodes to the overall framework(s) of a story is the most important way of grasping the unity of the narrative and the best antidote to the fragmentation that weakens so many discussions of biblical stories.

One of the most crucial of all rules for reading the stories of the Bible is therefore this one: *analyze in detail the unity of the story, noting how each episode relates to the overriding framework(s) and how the episodes relate to each other in the unfolding progress of the story.*

The interaction of setting, characters, and plot is the foundation of any story. There is, however,

Relating Individual Episodes to the Overriding Framework

much more to the dynamics of biblical narrative than this foundation. Biblical storytellers invariably make use of additional narrative devices.

The Test Motif in Stories

One of the commonest of all the strategies that storytellers use is to put the protagonist into situations that test him or her. Almost every major episode in the story of Abraham, for example, turns out to be a test of his faith. The story of Esther is organized around the test of the heroine's loyalty at a time of national crisis. King Saul's obedience to God is tested in the battles against the Philistines (1 Sam. 13:8–15) and the Amalekites (1 Sam. 15). Jesus' teachings and claims about himself are repeatedly tested by his antagonists in the Gospels.

Types of Tests: 1. Tests of Physical Strength or Courage

The tests of the hero can be of several types. Tests of physical strength and endurance, especially on the battlefield, have appealed most to storytellers through the centuries, and the Bible has its share of such stories. One thinks of the famous stories of David and Goliath, Samson and the Philistines, Jael and Sisera, Gideon and the Midianites.

2. Tests of Resourcefulness

Other stories test the hero's resourcefulness or cleverness. In the story of the stolen blessing (Gen. 27), Jacob's ability to trick his father is tested from the moment he enters his father's presence. Ehud's lefthanded trickiness is tested in the grim story of his assassination of Eglon (Judg. 3:15–30). David's resourcefulness is tested in such incidents as his flight from Saul and his capture by Achish, king of Gath (see 1 Sam. 21:10–15 for the latter).

3. Mental or Psychological Tests

Generally, though, biblical storytellers prefer more subtle types of tests than those involving physical strength or resourcefulness. One category is the mental or psychological testing of the protagonist. In the Old Testament, the hero with an ability to interpret dreams is the counterpart of the modern detective who can solve ingenious crimes. Other types of inner testing are also common in the Bible. For example, Joseph's willingness to forgive his brothers and conquer his impulse to take revenge is sorely tested when his brothers show up in Egypt. Elijah's ability to persist in his calling as a prophet is tested when Jezebel threatens to kill him

(1 Kings 19). Job's patience is tested in his suffering, while the ability of Moses to withstand the pressure of adverse public opinion is repeatedly tested in the story of the Exodus. Many a biblical hero finds his or her courage tested by threatening situations.

The most profound type of testing is moral or spiritual. We think at once of Potiphar's wife tempting Joseph to commit adultery with her, or Daniel's dilemma when the command to worship the emperor is published, or David's fiasco with Bathsheba and Uriah, or Satan's temptation of Jesus. What is tested in such stories is the protagonist's faith in God or obedience to God's moral law.

4. Moral or Spiritual Tests

The test motif is pervasive in the stories of the Bible. Whenever it is present, it is a good framework for organizing the story. Usually it is also a key to the story's meaning.

A related feature of stories is that they focus on the choices of the characters in the story. Stories concentrate on the person at the crossroads. Consequently, many stories are structured around the threefold principle of the antecedents, occurrence, and consequences of a crucial choice. The story of Esther is a good example. For three chapters we read about a series of events that finally converge to put Esther in the critical position of being the only one who can appeal to the king to save her nation. Chapter 4 focuses on her heroic choice to risk herself for her nation. The rest of the story suspensefully narrates how she gradually carries through on her choice to confront the king, and on what happens when she does.

The Centrality of Choice in Stories

Many a biblical protagonist achieves full heroic stature in the moment of choice. The choice, indeed, is what the story is finally about. We can recall Abraham choosing to leave his native land in obedience to the call of God, or his later choosing to obey God's command to sacrifice Isaac. We remember Moses refusing to be called the son of Pharaoh's daughter and choosing to identify with the Israelites, or Ruth choosing to stay with Naomi, or Daniel's three friends refusing to bow down to the emperor's statue, or Jesus choosing to submit to God's will in the Garden of Gethsemane.

Choice as the Heroic Act

The prominence of testing and choice in the stories of the Bible has a corresponding rule for reading and discussing them: *identify the exact nature of the tests that protagonists undergo or the choices they make, observing how the story is structured around these tests or choices and noting how leading themes of the story are related to testing and choice.*

Transformation as a Narrative Principle

It is characteristic of stories that they do not end where they began. Change, growth, and development are the very essence of stories. Without some type of change in character or situation, stories bore us. In fact, one expert on stories theorizes that a "minimal story" consists of "three events, the third of which is the inverse of the first."[10] Aristotle's principle of a story as an action having a beginning, middle, and end will serve us well here. The middle of the story is that which links the beginning and end and explains the difference that we find between the two situations. That difference nearly always centers on some notable change, usually one that involves the hero.

Change in the Story of Origins

Consider the very first story in the Bible, the story of origins that occupies Genesis 1–3. According to C. S. Lewis this story "fulfills the conditions of great story better perhaps than any other, for, more than any other, it leaves things where it did not find them."[11] The story begins with God's creation of a perfect world. Then the action narrows to life in Paradise (Gen. 2). The third chapter reverses everything. Life inside the Garden is replaced by life outside the Garden, in a fallen and hostile environment. Unity among God, humanity, and nature is transformed into a world fragmented into warring components. As we read through the first three chapters of the Bible, we fall from the zenith of total bliss to the absolute nadir of corrupting sin.

---

[10]Gerald Prince, *A Grammar of Stories* (The Hague: Mouton, 1973), 28.

[11]*A Preface to Paradise Lost* (New York: Oxford University Press, 1942), 133. Lewis makes the claim for Milton's treatment of the biblical story in *Paradise Lost*.

The element of change is so central to stories that the best system for classifying stories is based on it. The change in a story can be a change of (a) fortune or situation, (b) character, or (c) a combination of these. The resulting taxonomy of narrative types, with three biblical examples of each, looks something like this, beginning with stories in which the change is one of external fortune.

In a *tragic plot* an essentially good character undergoes a catastrophic change of fortune caused by his or her tragic flaw (the stories of Adam, Saul, Samson). A *punitive plot* is one in which an unsympathetic or villainous character undergoes an adverse change of fortune as a punishment for misdeeds (the stories of Jezebel, Ahab, Absalom). In a *pathetic plot* (from the word "pathos") a sympathetic character undergoes suffering or adversity through no particular fault of his or her own (the stories of Joseph, Job, Jesus). A *comic plot* is one in which a sympathetic character undergoes a change from misfortune or deprivation to happiness and fulfillment, or who survives the threat of misfortune and comes out all right in the end (the stories of Abraham, Ruth, Esther). A combination of pathetic and comic plots is possible if the suffering protagonist experiences a sudden upturn of fortune at the end (in contrast to the gradually improving fortunes of the protagonist in the typical comic plot). An *admiration story* is one in which a sympathetic hero successfully masters one threat after another (stories of heroes who always win, such as those of Daniel, Deborah, Elisha).

Stories in which the transformation is primarily a change of the protagonist's character yield a different system of classification. In *reform stories* an initially unsympathetic or evil character changes for the better (the stories of Jacob, Saul/Paul, the prodigal son). In *degeneration plots* an initially good and sympathetic character degenerates (the stories of Adam and Eve, Solomon, Hezekiah). In *revelation stories* the focus is on the protagonist's progress from ignorance to knowledge (the story of Abraham, who pursues several dead ends while learning how and when God will fulfill the promise of a son; the story of Job, who learns a great deal about God and himself as a result of his suffering; the story of David/Bathsheba/Uriah in 2 Sam. 11–12, where David gradually learns that not even the king can sin with impunity).

This classification of stories should be used flexibly. It does not cover every story told in the Bible. Some stories combine features of more than one type and should therefore be regarded as hybrids. For example, in the Bible (but not in literature generally) tragic stories are always degeneration stories as well. The story types I have listed are simply useful organizing frameworks for some biblical stories. They are not a literary straitjacket into which we should force every story. I leave it to my readers to discover that there are surprisingly few examples of some of these types and a notable abundance of other types.

We can formulate this further rule for reading and discussing biblical narrative on the basis of narrative transformation: *pay attention to the changes that occur between the beginning and end of a story, noting carefully the precise ways in which characters change and the causes of those transformations.*

Foils

Storytellers make significant use of foils in stories. A foil is literally something that "sets off" or heightens what is most important in a story. It is usually a *contrast*, though it can also consist of a *parallel* that reinforces something else. The commonest type of foil is a character who accentuates the protagonist, but sometimes an event or thread of action can serve as a foil to the main plot.

Characters as Foils

Character foils occur in almost every biblical narrative. The virtuous Abel heightens the villainy of Cain. Ruth's loyalty to her mother-in-law stands illumined by the contrast to Orpah, who returns to her home and gods. The roll call of such character foils keeps expanding: Abraham and Lot, Jacob and Esau, Rachel and Leah, David and Saul, Mary and Martha, the Pharisee and publican.

Contrasting Events as Foils

Events can also function as foils. In Genesis 18, Abraham and Sarah entertain angelic visitors with ideal hospitality in a rural setting, and they are rewarded with the promise that their long-awaited son will be born the following spring. In the very next chapter, the angels visit Lot to pronounce God's judgment against the wicked city of sexual perversion where Lot has made his home. Instead of sitting down to a leisurely meal, they have to be rescued from attempted homosexual rape. Again, in the story of Saul and David, the tragic decline of Saul stands silhouetted against the rise of the youthful David.

Plots can also be highlighted by parallel events that reinforce a main action. The story of Jacob provides good examples. The sibling rivalry Jacob perpetrated so well in his own childhood home is reinforced by the rivalry between Rachel and Leah after they become the wives of Jacob. Jacob's character flaws as the deceitful trickster are all the more obvious when he is thrown into a twenty-year-long encounter with his equally tricky Uncle Laban.

Parallel Events as Foils

Storytellers love to work with heightened contrasts and (less often) parallels. By means of such foils, they draw our attention to what is most important in the story.

Storytellers are also addicted to a narrative device known as dramatic irony. It occurs whenever the reader knows something that a character in the story does not know.

Dramatic Irony

For example, we read the Gospels knowing that the story ends with the resurrection of Jesus from the dead. The Gospel writers wrote their accounts from the superior (postresurrection) knowledge that Jesus was the Messiah. But as we go through the action narrated in the Gospels, we can discern irony all over the place as the disciples and enemies of Jesus portrayed in the story operate in ignorance of who Jesus is and of his ultimate triumph.

Irony in the Gospels

The most sustained piece of dramatic irony in the Bible is the Book of Job. As readers, we know from the prologue that God is not the cause of Job's suffering (Satan is), that Job is blameless and upright, and that God is not punishing Job. The principal actors operate in ignorance of what has happened in heaven, and almost everything they say is permeated with dramatic irony. As we read Job's early speeches we know that Job's accusations against God as a sadistic deity are untrue. In

Irony in the Story of Job

the speeches of Job's "comforters" we observe the irony of orthodoxy: they mouth orthodox doctrine (suffering is punitive, wicked people bring calamity on themselves, God is just), but all this orthodoxy is wide of the mark because it does not apply to the specific case of Job.

Localized Irony

Dramatic irony is usually more localized than it is in the Gospels and the Book of Job. Much of the emotional voltage of the concluding chapters of the story of Joseph stems from our knowing, as the brothers do not, that they are unwittingly fulfilling the destiny prophesied in Joseph's youthful dreams. Again, since we know that the crafty, lefthanded Ehud carries his sword on the unexpected right side, the storyteller in effect exchanges a grim wink with us at the expense of the doomed Eglon, with the result that virtually every detail in the story (Judg. 3:15–25) is electrified with hidden meanings. In a famous story from the New Testament we hear the approaching footsteps of the young men returning from the burial of Ananias even as we listen to Sapphira's doomed attempt to pull off the same hoax that cost her husband his life (Acts 5:7–10).

Dramatic Irony and Reader Involvement

Dramatic irony is one of the most predictably effective ways of eliciting reader involvement in a story. It activates a reader to recognize a discrepancy. Once activated, we are "hooked." This may account for the fact that it is hard to find a story that does not include some irony, however subtle. But in the Bible irony is more than a bit of effective storytelling technique. In a universe where God's ways transcend human understanding and in which an unseen spiritual world is portrayed as being just as real as the physical world, it is inevitable that discrepancies in perception will keep entering the action.[12]

Poetic Justice

Poetic justice is also common in stories. It consists of the narrative situation in which good characters are rewarded and bad ones punished. Such justice is what we usually get in biblical stories before the final curtain closes on the action.

---

[12]A particularly excellent treatment of irony in the Bible is Edwin M. Good's book *Irony in the Old Testament* (Philadelphia: Westminster, 1965).

The boy-hero David triumphs and the blasphemous giant loses his head. The villainous Haman is hanged on the gallows that he himself built, while Mordecai basks in his promotion. Job's fortunes are restored, his tormenting "friends" are rebuked, and Satan has fled from the scene in total defeat.

Such poetic justice is all but inevitable in stories. As readers, we intuitively expect it, even though we recognize that such justice is often absent in real life. Poetic justice is simply one of the conventions of storytelling. It is a way to round off an action with a note of finality (without it storytellers would hardly know how to end their stories). It is the storyteller's way of clarifying how he feels morally and perhaps emotionally about the characters and events that have been presented, and, to use Aristotle's great phrase, it satisfies our moral sense.

Is the prevalence of poetic justice in the stories of the Bible a sign that the writers have added a bit of fiction to make the story "turn out right"? It is more likely to be a matter of selecting stories that *did* turn out right. After all, what type of story gets told and retold in our own culture? And what type of story is offered as a testimony of God's goodness or as the prototypical Christian life? Stories in which justice wins, good people are rewarded, and scoundrels get their comeuppance. In the Bible, poetic justice is more appropriately called God's justice.

The prevalence of such standard narrative conventions as foils, dramatic irony, and poetic justice in the stories of the Bible can be formulated into a principle of interpretation: *be alert for the presence of foils, dramatic irony, and poetic justice in biblical narrative, both for what they add to your response to the story and what they contribute to the meaning.*

The storytellers of the Bible do more than entertain us. They interpret as well as present the characters and events that make up their stories.

Why Storytellers Use Poetic Justice

SUMMARY

Stories Are Comments on Life

"To tell a story," writes John Shea, "is to create a world, adopt an attitude, suggest a behavior."[13] Storytellers even *choose* their stories partly on the basis of their significance and ability to embody truth. They are always on the lookout for stories that are striking and gripping, but they also choose stories in which, to use the French writer Baudelaire's words, "the deep significance of life reveals itself."[14]

The fact that storytellers *mean* something by their stories affects how we should approach their stories. A leading literary scholar speaks of "the rule of significance" as "the primary convention of literature"; by the rule of significance he means reading a work of literature "as expressing a significant attitude to some problem concerning man and/or his relation to the universe."[15] In reading the stories of the Bible we need to balance the descriptive question "What happened next?" with the interpretive questions "What does it mean? What is the author driving at?" At both levels, stories are at least a distant literary relative of the riddle, teasing us into a process of discovery.

What Stories Are About

The rule of significance is especially relevant to the Bible, a sacred or religious book in which the authors claim to be revealing religious truth for the faith and practice of their readers. We should look upon biblical stories as making implied assertions about the three great issues of life:

1. Reality: What really exists?
2. Morality: What constitutes good and bad behavior?
3. Values: What really matters, and what matters most?

Biblical storytellers make these assertions, not directly, but by embodying them in setting, character, and action. Flannery O'Connor once remarked

---

[13]*Stories of God* (Chicago: Thomas More, 1978), 9.

[14]Quoted by J. Middleton Murry, *The Problem of Style* (London: Oxford University Press, 1922), 30.

[15]Jonathan Culler, *Structuralist Poetics* (Ithaca: Cornell University Press, 1975), 115.

that the storyteller speaks *"with* character and
action, not *about* character and action."[16] If this is
true, *about* what to do storytellers speak by means
of their stories? The same thing other thinkers
speak about more directly: life, reality, truth.
There is, in other words, a *discourse level* to these
stories: they are the *means by which* the author
communicates something important to the audience
or reader.

There is an obvious indirection about the storyteller's approach to truth. Instead of stating ideas
propositionally, the storyteller presents living examples of one principle or another, one aspect of
reality or another, leaving the reader to infer those
themes. In other words, stories impose the obligation of interpretation on their readers in a way that
sermons and essays do not.

The Need to Interpret Stories

How, then, can the reader know what a given
story *means*? Readers do not always agree on what
a story means, though often it is possible to find a
consensus. Keeping in mind that the storyteller
both *presents* an experience and offers an *interpretation* of it, we can profitably pursue our quest to
find the themes of a story by dividing the process
into two phases: identifying *what* the story is about
(the topic or subject of the story) and *how* the
writer wishes us to view the experience that is
presented (the theme of the story).

The Dual Task in Interpreting Stories

The most reliable guide to what a story is about
is the principle of repetition. What keeps getting
repeated in a story invariably becomes the central
focus—the thing toward which everything points.
The most important requirement for a story, com-
mented the Russian novelist Leo Tolstoy, "is that
it should have a kind of focus, . . .some place
where all the rays meet or from which they
issue."[17] Such focus is usually provided by repetition. Generally speaking, a story will partly interpret itself by repeating that which is essential to its
understanding.

Repetition as a Guide to What a Story Is About

---

[16]*Mystery and Manners*, 76.

[17]*Talks with Tolstoy*, as excerpted in *Novelists on the
Novel*, ed. Miriam Allott (London: Routledge and Kegan
Paul, 1959), 235.

Repetition in the Story of Gideon

For example, in the first half of the story of Gideon (Judg. 6–7), virtually every incident is a variation on the theme of the hero's feelings of inadequacy. Gideon beats out wheat in secret to avoid detection (6:11). When the angel ironically greets him as "thou mighty man of valour" (v. 12 KJ), Gideon responds with defeatism (v. 13). When God promises to be with him, he asks for a confirming sign (vv. 16–18). Given the command to tear down his father's pagan altar, Gideon does it by night "because he was too afraid of his family and the men of the town to do it by day" (v. 27). This story, we quickly learn, is going to be about what God did with a reluctant hero suffering from acute insecurity.

Highlighting or Foregrounding

In addition to repetition as a device to tell us what a story is about, biblical storytellers use various techniques of highlighting or foregrounding to direct a reader's attention to what is most important in a story. Anything that stands out from a common ground can become a signpost for the reader.

Character Transformation as a Form of Highlighting

In a story that centers on character transformation, for example, we rather automatically pay attention to what caused the transformation. The story of Esther is typical. During the early part of the story, Esther conceals her Jewish identity and fits in perfectly with a pagan lifestyle. After her crucial decision in the middle of the story to unmask her concealed identity before the king, she becomes a national heroine, no longer sliding with circumstances and taking the easiest way out of a situation. What is the story about? It is about the identity crisis of the protagonist, an identity crisis very much tied up with the religious themes of the Old Testament.

Proportionate Space as a Form of Highlighting

Highlighting can consist of the amount of space that a given detail or event gets in a story. In the Greek text of the parable of the good Samaritan, for example, "there are forty-six words given to what precedes the arrival of the Samaritan on the scene but sixty words devoted to his arrival and, step-by-step, to his reaction. Since this reaction is so unexpected, it must be spelled out in explicit detail."[18]

There is an alternative to a writer's using proportionate space to highlight the central feature of a story, and that is to throw a relatively small facet of a story into relief by making it the crucial or decisive aspect. Jacob's wrestling with the angel at the brook Jabbok (Gen. 32:22–32) takes only eleven verses to tell, but it is the great turning point in Jacob's story and the clue to what the storyteller wishes us to see in the story as a whole. In terms of sheer space, the aggressive selfishness of Jacob is far more dominant, but the prolonged account of Jacob the scoundrel exists only as the background against which the main point of the story stands silhouetted.

Crucial or Decisive Events as a Form of Highlighting

The story of Ruth contains a similar instance of a small detail that gets foregrounded. Near the end of the story, we find the ostensibly matter-of-fact statement that the child born to Ruth and Boaz was named "Obed. He was the father of Jesse, the father of David" (Ruth 4:17). In terms of space, it is of only passing interest, but as Ronald Hals comments, with the mere mention of David "the story of Ruth takes its place as simply one more bit of *Heilsgeschichte* ["sacred history"], for it clearly aims to trace the background of the great David. In fact, the story could well be described as messianic history."[19]

Once we have discovered what a biblical story is about (and it might be about more than one thing), we need to complete the task of interpretation by determining exactly what the storyteller says about and with that subject matter. What perspective are we invited to share with the storyteller? To use the terminology of literary criticism, what point of view governs the writer's account of the characters and action in the story? The answers to these questions are multiple.

Point of View in Stories

---

[18]John Dominic Crossan, *The Dark Interval: Towards a Theology of Story* (Niles, Ill.: Argus Communications, 1975), 107–8.

[19]*The Theology of the Book of Ruth* (Philadelphia: Fortress, 1969), 19.

Authorial
Statement as a
Guide to Point
of View

Sometimes a biblical storyteller enters the story and directly states the interpretive framework that he intends us to apply to the story. When the writer of the Abraham story stops the flow of the action to state, "Abram believed the LORD, and he credited it to him as righteousness" (Gen. 15:6), the editorial comment presents a major theme of the whole story, namely, the reward that attends faith in God. When we read later in Genesis that "the LORD was with Joseph and shewed him mercy" (Gen. 39:21 KJ), we know that the providential theme is a main meaning of the story. What is the controlling theme that underlies the Gospel of John? The writer himself tells us: "These are written that you may believe that Jesus is the Christ, the Son of God" (John 20:31).

Scarcity of
Authorial
Statement

Although such authorial commentary does occur in the stories of the Bible, the significant thing is how rarely it happens compared to what we find in stories outside the Bible. Generally speaking, biblical storytellers narrate what happened but do not explain it.

Normative
Characters
Within Stories

It is much more common to find that characters within the stories of the Bible make key utterances that we intuitively recognize as summing up what the story as a whole is asserting. At the end of the Joseph story, Joseph himself suggests an interpretive framework for the whole story when he tells his brothers, "As for you, you meant evil against me; but God meant it for good, to bring it about that many people should be kept alive" (Gen. 50:20). This providential theme of the victory of redemptive suffering over intended evil is at the very heart of what the story communicates. Whenever a character in a story interprets the meaning of the story in this way, we can call both the character and the viewpoint *normative* (authoritative). The Gospel stories are filled with such normative spokespersons, such as the centurion in the Passion story who exclaims, "Surely he was the Son of God!" (Matt. 27:54).

God as
Normative
Spokesman

In the Bible there is a special category of normative characters. In many stories God or, in the Gospels, Jesus makes a stated or implied comment on the meaning of the action. The pattern begins with the story of the Fall in Genesis 3, where God enters the action to pronounce judgment against Adam and Eve for their disobedience. Thereafter the appearance of God as a normative character is the rule rather than the exception in Old Testament stories. A similar pattern pervades the Gospel narratives, where the stories involving Jesus typically include some pronouncement by Jesus about the meaning of an episode.

The point of view in most biblical stories is conveyed, not by explicit statements from either the storyteller or normative characters within the stories, but in a more indirect manner. More often than not, the persuasive or interpretive strategy in biblical narrative is embodied within the details of the stories. It is up to the reader to read the interpretive signals accurately.

The Typical Indirectness of Authorial Viewpoint

Authorial selectivity and arrangement of details lie behind every story in the Bible. There is always more than one way to tell a given story. The story as it finally stands has been consciously assembled by the author for a calculated effect on the audience. In short, storytellers control what you see and don't see, how you see it, and when you see it.

Selectivity as a Form of Authorial Viewpoint

We can take the story of David to show authorial selectivity as a way of influencing how readers interpret a story. David's story is included in three different Old Testament works. In 1 and 2 Samuel, the writer puts the first part of David's life into a providential framework of God's favor toward the hero, and he includes events that idealize David. Then all of a sudden in 2 Samuel 11–12 we get the Bathsheba/Uriah debacle, accompanied by God's judgment. The rest of the story becomes a detailed anatomy of the misery that followed in the wake of David's great sin. The writer has obviously given David's life a tragic interpretation.

Controlling What You See and Don't See

But in 1 Kings (e.g., 9:4; 11:4, 6; 15:3) David appears as a norm of the godly ruler against which evil kings are weighed and found wanting. Even more striking is the picture in 1 Chronicles, which tells us both more and less than the Books of Samuel. Here we find six chapters describing David's gathering of materials for the temple and his arrangements for temple worship, and seven chapters devoted to the hero's military exploits. We hear nothing, however, about the Bathsheba/Uriah episode. This selectivity gives us a heroic interpretation of David's life, with emphasis on his piety and courage and national accomplishments.

Character Portrayal as a Conscious Interpretation by the Writer

The fact that David emerges as a partly different person in the various accounts shows that writers influence how we interpret characters and action simply by what they choose to include and exclude. Characters in biblical stories are conscious creations of the storytellers, not in the sense that the writers disregard the real-life person, but in the sense that they decide what to include and exclude from their portrait. Just as people in real life elicit more than one response and assessment from those who know them, biblical writers do not all see a given character in exactly the same way. We are here talking about the multiplicity of a character, not questioning the reliability of a storyteller. David's life *was* both tragic and heroic.

Point of View in the Gospels

The Gospels are an even more famous example of how a biblical storyteller's very selection of material results in an interpretation of the character and events that make up the story. Biblical scholars have established in detail how each of the Gospels tells the story of Jesus from its own perspective, and that this viewpoint is discernible in large part in what each author decided to include in his account. Luke, for example, included a number of distinctive incidents and teachings of Jesus that involve the poor, women, and non-Jewish people (especially Samaritans) that are absent from the other Gospels. This selectivity reflects an interpretation of the person and mission of Jesus.

Selectivity in the Hagar Story

Selectivity can also produce more localized effects in stories. Consider, for instance, the way in which we respond to Hagar and her son Ishmael in Genesis 21. The relative illegitimacy of Ishmael and his exclusion from the covenant line are underscored by his antagonism toward Isaac, the true child of promise (vv. 8–10). If this antagonism and the expulsion of Hagar and Ishmael were all that was included in the story, our impression would be one of simple condemnation. But the storyteller includes more than that. He elicits our pity for the mother and child wandering in the desert (vv. 15–16), and he lends a kind of sanction to them by including God's rescue of Hagar and his words of kindness to her (vv. 17–20). If we had only the first half of this story, our final assessment of the characters and events would be far different from what they are now.

All of this leads to an important principle of narrative interpretation: *assume that the storyteller has included every detail for a purpose, and do not hesitate to reflect on how the story is affected by the inclusion of a detail as compared with the effect if the detail were omitted.*

As readers we are influenced not only by what we see and don't see (the writer's selectivity), but also by the arrangement of the material. Most important of all is the way in which a story ends. One of the inherent principles of narrative is the idea of outcome. If characters in stories undertake an experiment in living, then the outcome of that experiment is an implied comment on its adequacy or inadequacy. It is in this context that the narrative convention of poetic justice makes most sense. Why do most biblical stories end with poetic justice? Because it is a way for a storyteller to indicate his own world view and system of moral values.

The Ending of a Story as an Implied Comment on Its Meaning

Almost any story in the Bible will illustrate the way in which the outcome of the story casts a retrospective interpretation over the preceding action. In Genesis 13 we read about the parting of the ways of Abraham and Lot and the different types of life to which they commit themselves. It is the type of crossroads experience that calls for a sequel. This is exactly what we get several chapters later, where Lot's life degenerates into a sordid end, while Abraham's life blossoms into a life of spiritual and domestic blessing. In the same story, Abraham and Sarah's decision to have a child by the maid Hagar leads to problems, both immediately and throughout subsequent Jewish history. That outcome influences how we interpret Abraham's venture in expediency. Ruth risks herself by choosing a new nation and a new God, and the conclusion of the story shows the reward that was hers.

Endings in Biblical Stories

King Saul decides to win popularity with the people by following a path of expediency instead of obeying God and comes to a tragic end.

The accompanying rule for interpreting biblical stories is an important one: *look upon the conclusion of a story as an implied comment on (evaluation of) the characters and events that the story has presented.*

Influencing a Reader's Sympathy and Aversion

Much of the rhetorical or persuasive strategy of biblical storytellers consists of getting readers to respond to characters and events in a designed way. At its very heart, narrative is a form in which authors influence their readers to respond with either sympathy or aversion to what happens in the story. A literary scholar who made a thorough study of the "devices of disclosure" by which selected storytellers influenced how readers interpret the ethical meaning of their stories concluded that the meaning of a story "depended heavily on how successful its creator was in controlling our sympathy and antipathy toward, approval and disapproval of, characters, thoughts, and actions at every stage."[20]

The reader of the stories in the Bible has a special advantage in this regard. The stories of the Bible are embedded in a much larger book that contains an abundance of explicitly didactic and doctrinal material. The overtly didactic parts of the Bible are a constant frame of reference by which to evaluate characters and events in the stories of Scripture.

Sympathy and Aversion in the Story of Naboth's Vineyard

We can use the story of Naboth and his vineyard (1 Kings 21:1–16) as an example of how the meaning of a story depends on the way in which the author manages to guide our sympathy and aversion toward the characters and events in the story. The first thing that secures our sympathy toward Naboth is his religious reason for refusing to relinquish his vineyard (v. 3). With the double reference to "the inheritance of my fathers" (vv. 3, 4) our minds reach back to the Mosaic stipulations regarding land as a sacred trust of the family that had originally received it (Lev. 25:13–28; Num.

[20]Sheldon Sacks, *Fiction and the Shape of Belief* (Berkeley: University of California Press, 1964), 249.

36:9). King Ahab, by contrast, elicits our disdain by his sullenness, his irreligious insensitivity to the Mosaic law, and his childish pouting (v. 4). Queen Jezebel quickly emerges as even more shocking to our moral sensibilities. Her intrigue against the innocent Naboth violates both universal moral norms and biblical moral commands. As readers we protest every inch of the way as she manipulates the helpless Naboth, hires perjured witnesses, cruelly engineers the stoning of an innocent man, and callously tells Ahab to take possession of the vineyard. Even if we did not have the benefit of Elijah's pronouncement of God's judgment in the verses immediately following, we would know what this gripping story means.

Stories are *affective* by their very nature. They draw us into an encounter with characters and events to which we inevitably respond. Someone has said that "the writer expresses what he knows by affecting the reader; the reader knows what is expressed by being receptive to effects. The medium of this process is language."[21] Responses can, of course, be ill-informed or simply wrong, but we will do a better job of interpreting the meaning of stories, both in the Bible and beyond it, if we pay attention to how the characters and events affect us, whether sympathetically or unsympathetically. Stories convey their meanings partly by influencing the reader's responses to events and situations.

The rule of interpretation that follows from the affective nature of narrative is this: *pay attention to how a story influences your approval and disapproval of events and characters, and formulate a statement of what the story means on the basis of this approval pattern.*

We know from disagreements among readers that some biblical stories remain ambiguous or controversial (usually in part rather than as a whole) when this rule of reader response is applied to them. But the overwhelming majority of biblical stories will yield a clear interpretation based on a reader's response to characters and events. It is true that biblical storytellers preserve the mystery

Stories Communicate by Affecting

The Clarity of Biblical Narrative

---

[21]David Lodge, *Language of Fiction* (London: Routledge and Kegan Paul, 1966), 65.

of human character and supernatural reality, but their implied assertions about reality, morality, and values are clear. Their stories conform to novelist Joyce Cary's theory that "all writers. . .must have, to compose any kind of story, some picture of the world, and of what is right and wrong in that world," and that good writers insure that "a reader. . .never be left in doubt about the meaning of a story."[22] Of course, if modern readers disregard what the Bible says about reality, morality, and values in its doctrinal parts, they will naturally blur the focus that biblical storytellers have built into their stories. But that will be the fault of the reader, not the writer.

SUMMARY   The sheer quantity of "rules" for reading and interpreting biblical stories may seem overwhelming. If so, may I say that these principles are not a list that anyone needs to memorize. They are simply rules of storytelling and interpretation that we should be ready to apply when the occasion arises. We tend to apply most of these rules intuitively, simply as close readers of the biblical text. But most of us can sharpen our ability to read biblical stories by being more systematic than we usually are.

A brief checklist of the narrative elements that require scrutiny looks something like this:

1. Physical, temporal, and cultural settings in a story.
2. Characters in the story, with special emphasis on the protagonist.
3. Plot conflicts and their resolution.
4. Aspects of narrative suspense (how the story arouses curiosity about outcome).
5. The protagonist's experiment in living as an implied comment about life.
6. Narrative unity, coherence, and emphasis.
7. Elements of testing and choice in the story.
8. Character progress and transformation.
9. Foils, dramatic irony, and poetic justice.

---

[22]*Art and Reality* (New York: Harper and Brothers, 1958), 158, 114.

10. The implied assertions about reality, morality, and values.
11. Repetition and highlighting as clues to what the story is about.
12. Point of view in the story—how the writer gets a reader to share his attitude toward the characters and events.

To bring all of this into focus, I wish to apply these principles to the story of Esau's selling of his birthright to his brother Jacob. The story is this (Gen. 25:27–34):

The Story of the Birthright as a Test Case

> [27]The boys grew up, and Esau became a skillful hunter, a man of the open country, while Jacob was a quiet man, staying among the tents.
> [28]Isaac, who had a taste for wild game, loved Esau, but Rebekah loved Jacob.
> [29]Once when Jacob was cooking some stew, Esau came in from the open country, famished. [30]He said to Jacob, "Quick, let me have some of that red stew! I'm famished!" (That is why he was also called Edom.)
> [31]Jacob replied, "First sell me your birthright."
> [32]"Look, I am about to die," Esau said. "What good is the birthright to me?"
> [33]But Jacob said, "Swear to me first." So he swore an oath to him, selling his birthright to Jacob.
> [34]Then Jacob gave Esau some bread and some lentil stew. He ate and drank, and then got up and left. So Esau despised his birthright.

The experiential realism of biblical narrative is fully evident in this brief story. Here is a story that turns upon a pot of stew. As is so often the case in the Bible, a thoroughly mundane event becomes invested with a sense of ultimate spiritual destiny. The story revolves, moreover, around sibling rivalry and as such awakens our own experience of that archetypal phenomenon. It is the type of story that is thoroughly rooted in familiar everyday reality.

The Experiential Realism of the Story

The first two verses give us the background information that is essential to understand the story that follows. These verses introduce the grand foil or contrast around which the story is built. It is the spectacle of twin brothers with opposite temperaments and lifestyles. The outdoor hunter favored by his father is contrasted to his quiet and domestic

Foils in the Story

brother, who of course is the mother's favorite. The opening contrast is so pronounced that we could predict conflict between the two brothers even before the plot of the story unfolds. This seething pot of sibling rivalry produces the central action of the story.

The Setting of the Story

The setting for the action at once gives Jacob the advantage. The tent is his natural environment. Esau, by contrast, is out of his depth in this setting. A pot of stew becomes a weapon in the hands of the family cook. A person as governed by his physical appetites as Esau proves to be is no match for a schemer like Jacob. The situation is one that we have seen dozens of times on television and in life: the gullible dupe waiting to be taken by the clever trickster. Our narrative curiosity about outcome is assured by the very situation.

Plot Conflict and Reversal of Situation

The conflict that underlies this story of sibling rivalry is the struggle to secure the benefits represented by the birthright. The situation—bartering between hostile persons—has conflict written all over it. In this conflict Jacob is the protagonist, the aggressive manipulator who initiates the action and dominates his brother. His chief strategy for getting the upper hand in the struggle is to put Esau in a position that tests him. With the smell of pottage in his nostrils, Esau is easy game. In six short verses, the opening situation is exactly reversed. The plot conflict is resolved as we watch the birthright change ownership and the brothers' respective fortunes reversed in that very exchange. As so often in biblical narrative, the significance of what happens is all out of proportion to the actual brevity of the story. By this single act of bartering, both Jacob and Esau have made a life-changing choice.

Unity and Coherence

Every detail in the story contributes to the unifying action of the exchanged birthright. At the end of the story Esau leaves the scene with a full stomach and without the birthright. He does so because Jacob made him swear to give him the birthright. This sale, in turn, occurred because Esau had asked for food. He had asked for food when he had come home hungry just as Jacob was cooking dinner. This is obviously a cause-effect sequence of events having a beginning, middle, and end.

What about the characters in the story? They are known to us through their words and actions. Jacob is above all the clever schemer. His cleverness is seen mainly in his ability to seize the opportune moment and to turn it to his advantage, and in his making Esau swear an oath to make the bargain binding, lest Esau later change his mind. Other traits also emerge from Jacob's actions: he is aggressive, devious, unfair (even though he does not literally steal the birthright), unloving, unscrupulous in exploiting another person for his own advantage, and materialistic (the birthright assured him of a double portion of the inheritance).

Techniques of Characterization

Esau comes off even worse in the story. He lives only for the moment. He cannot endure a little discomfort for the sake of future benefit. He has no capacity for grasping the covenant promises and spiritual blessings that would accompany this particular birthright.

What does the story communicate at the level of theme or meaning? Patterns of repetition and the presence of a central character foil draw attention to two main themes. Esau's experiment in living focuses our attention on the question of values. The story is a memorable example of someone who chooses the lesser over the greater—immediate physical gratification over future blessing. Our proverb about "selling one's birthright for a mess of pottage" means exactly what the story does. The Anchor Bible renders the last sentence of the story, "Thus did Esau misprize his birthright," suggesting the inverted values by which Esau operates in the episode. Hebrews 12:16 provides a good interpretive framework for the story when it calls Esau "godless" or "profane" (KJ), having no adequate feeling for what is sacred.

What Is the Story About?

When we shift the spotlight from Esau to Jacob, the thing that keeps getting repeated in the story is his unbrotherly behavior. Here the story becomes a comment about morality rather than values. The portrait of Jacob in this story is a memorable and frightening picture of what selfishness can do to human relationships.

The Moral Aspect of the Story

Point of View
in the Story

How does the storyteller get us to share his negative assessment of both brothers' behavior? Like other biblical storytellers, he pays us the compliment of assuming that our own morality and sense of values are healthy. He depends partly on our negative responses to bad behavior in getting his point across.

The Outcome
as an Implied
Comment

He also uses the outcome of the story to convey his meaning. In the case of Jacob, we have to wait for subsequent episodes to see how destructive of self and family his experiment in self-serving proved to be. The verdict on Esau, by contrast, occurs within the story itself, and it takes two forms. One is the storyteller's final interpretive comment: "So Esau despised his birthright." In case we were in any doubt, this parting shot tells us what the action shows about Esau's inverted values.

Esau's Uncouth
Speech
Patterns

Along with this direct evaluation, the storyteller secures a negative response to Esau by stressing his uncouth lack of manners and vulgar personality. According to one commentator, in verse 30 "Esau is depicted as an uncouth glutton; he speaks of 'swallowing, gulping down,' instead of eating."[23] A good translation of what Esau says to Jacob in verse 30 would be, "Let me gulp some of that red stuff." To accentuate the importance of what is happening, the author tells us in the same verse that Esau's uncomplimentary nickname "Red" could be traced right back to this decisive event in his life. All of this is reinforced by the second half of verse 34, which "presents a staccato succession of five verbal forms . . . calculated to point up Esau's lack of manners and judgment."

The Total
Impact of the
Story

In a well-told story like this, everything works together to produce a unified impact. Form and meaning are inseparable. The sheer mastery of storytelling technique elicits our interest and delight, and at the same time we sense the significance of what happens in the story. We resonate with the story partly because it is simply good story material, memorable for its strong characters, its

---

[23]E. A. Speiser, *The Anchor Bible: Genesis* (Garden City: Doubleday, 1964), 195. I have used the same source for other material in this paragraph.

vivid situation, and its conflict whose resolution was so momentous in the lives of the actors. But we know that the storyteller also chose to tell the story for what it reveals about life. The story is a crucial chapter in salvation history and is simultaneously true to the way things are in the world. People still behave this way, and with the same dire results. We even have a proverb based on the story to prove it.

Further Reading

Literary Interpretations of Biblical Narratives, vols. 1, 2, ed. Kenneth R. R. Gros Louis (Nashville: Abingdon, 1974, 1982), contain numerous literary explications of biblical stories. In the first volume, D. F. Rauber's essay on the Book of Ruth (pp. 163–76) is a particularly outstanding model of what a literary analysis of a biblical story should be.

Robert C. Tannehill's article "The Disciples in Mark: The Function of a Narrative Role," *Journal of Religion* 57(1977):386–405, contains an abundance of good narrative theory that can be applied to biblical stories in general. Of a similar nature is Amos N. Wilder's essay "Story and Story-World," *Interpretation* 37(1983):353–64, which provides a brief overview of some of the leading "rituals of storytelling."

Jacob Licht, *Storytelling in the Bible* (Jerusalem: Magnes, 1978), is particularly helpful in anatomizing biblical stories into four narrative ingredients: straight narrative that merely tells what happened; scenic narrative, in which the action is broken up into dramatic scenes; description of scenes and characters; and explanatory commentary by the storyteller. Robert Alter does similar things in *The Art of Biblical Narrative* (New York: Basic Books, 1981).

Chapter Three

Types of
Biblical Stories

IN ADDITION TO THE GENERAL FEATURES of stories noted in the preceding chapter, there are a number of traits that are characteristic of more specialized narrative genres. These subtypes within the general category of narrative have their own procedures and rules of interpretation. Two of these subtypes, parable and gospel, will receive separate treatment in later chapters.

HEROIC NARRATIVE

The largest branch of narrative is heroic narrative. Hero stories are built around the life and exploits of a protagonist. Such stories spring from one of the most universal impulses of literature—the desire to embody accepted norms of behavior or representative struggles in the story of a character whose experience is typical of people in general.

A Definition of Heroic Narrative

The following definition of a literary hero is a good starting point for discussing heroic narrative:

Literary Heroes

A traditional. . .hero must be more than merely the leading figure or protagonist of a literary work. The true hero expresses an accepted social and moral norm; his experience reenacts the important conflicts of the community which produces him; he is endowed with qualities that capture the popular imagination. It must also be remarked that the hero is able to act, and to act for good. Most important of all, the narrative of his experience suggests that life has both a significant pattern and an end.[1]

The practical import of this definition is simple: both the dynamics of the action and the meanings the storyteller is trying to get across will be concentrated in the central hero. In interpreting a hero story, therefore, we cannot go wrong if we focus on the protagonist. The hero's conflicts and encounters comprise the plot of the story, and we can organize our understanding and discussion of the story around them.

Ways of Portraying a Hero

Determining the precise identity of a literary hero is a prime task whenever we read a heroic narrative. The hero's identity is revealed chiefly through six means: the hero's (1) personal traits and abilities, (2) actions, (3) motivations, (4) responses to events or people, (5) relationships, and (6) roles.

The Hero Is Representative of Humanity

A literary hero or heroine is representative. The purpose behind the storyteller's selection of specific heroes and events is that they in some sense capture the universal human situation. It is a commonplace that whereas the historian tells us what happened, the writer of literary narrative tells us what happens. The hero stories of the Bible do more than set the historical record straight. They are also models or paradigms of the religious experience of the human race. They capture what is true for us and for people around us. Characters like Joseph and Ruth and David do not stay within their stories in the Bible; they merge with our own experiences as we begin to "build bridges" between their stories and our own.

The Hero as an Ideal

Usually such representative heroes are exemplary of some ideal, though they need not be wholly good (in the Bible they rarely are completely idealized). Stories tend to get written about people whose character and exploits we can look up to. The stories of the Bible are no exception. They give us a memorable gallery of moral and spiritual models to emulate.

---

[1]Walter Houghton and G. Robert Stange, ed., *Victorian Poetry and Poetics* (Boston: Houghton Mifflin, 1968), xxiii.

On the other hand, stories can also inculcate a positive ideal by negative example. They can indirectly encourage good behavior by telling the story of a hero who failed to measure up to such a standard. Some of the most foolish misreadings of biblical stories I have encountered have come from a misguided assumption that we are intended to approve of the behavior of biblical heroes in virtually every episode in which they figure. One of the distinctive features of the Bible is how deeply flawed its heroes and heroines are. The Bible portrays most of its protagonists as Cromwell wished to be painted—warts and all.

Of course, in describing hero stories as moral or spiritual examples, I run the risk of making them appear to be simplistic moral fables. This is emphatically not true of heroic narrative in the Bible. All we need to do is dip into biblical scholarship and literary criticism to sense that these stories are subtle, frequently complex to interpret, and usually characterized by a kind of cryptic understatement or mystery that requires the reader to supply an abundance of interpretation. The moment we reduce the moral or spiritual meaning of the hero's experience to an idea, we have turned the story into a platitude and robbed it of its power.

The antidote lies in respecting how stories work. The values or virtues that are inculcated by a hero story like that of Joseph or Ruth are embodied in the protagonist's character and life. The strategy of literature is to give form and shape to human experience by projecting it onto a character. A story can communicate truth or reality or knowledge simply by picturing some aspect of human experience. A story conveys truth whenever we can say, "This is the way life is."

In other words, "the whole story is the meaning, because it is an experience, not an abstraction."[2] To say that the story of Abraham embodies an ideal of faith is not to offer that interpretation as a substitute for the story but as a pair of eyes by which to see what the story itself means. As

Conveying an Ideal by Negative Example

Hero Stories Are More Than Moral Fables

How Stories Picture Reality

---

[2]Flannery O'Connor, *Mystery and Manners,* ed. Sally and Robert Fitzgerald (New York: Farrar, Straus & Giroux, 1957), 73.

readers we must preserve the integrity of the story as a story, while at the same time realizing that "all narrative. . .possesses. . .some quality of parable."[3]

Questions to Ask of Hero Stories

Since a literary hero incarnates a society's views of reality, morality, and values, the following issues are good ones to explore when reflecting on hero stories.

1. The view of people. What kind of beings are people? How can people achieve meaning in life? What is the proper end or goal for a person? What is humanity's origin and what is its destination?

2. The religious view. Does the story postulate a transcendental realm? If so, what is its nature? How is the other world related to this world? How can a person be vitally related to God?

3. The view of society. What is the nature of the human community? What is the individual's role in society? What is the nature of the individual's obligations to his or her fellow humans?

4. The question of values. What does the story postulate as the highest value in life? Is it a person (God, self, some individual, people in general), an institution (state, church, home), an abstract quality (love, truth, beauty, order), or something physical like nature?

SUMMARY

Hero stories focus on the struggles and triumphs of the protagonist. The central hero or heroine is representative of a whole group and is usually a largely exemplary character, at least by the end of the story. The hero or heroine's destiny is an implied comment about life and reality.

EPIC

A Definition of Epic

Epic is a species within the class of heroic narrative. It is long narrative, a hero story on the grand scale. A single heroic narrative does not rate

[3]Frank Kermode, "Interpretive Continuities and the New Testament," *Raritan*, Spring 1982, 36.

as an epic because it lacks epic scope. Epic is an encyclopedic form that includes as much as possible. Northrop Frye calls it "the story of all things."[4] Epic is so expansive that it sums up a whole age; one scholar claims that "the supreme role of epic lies in its capacity to focus a society's self-awareness."[5]

As part of this expansiveness, epic always has a strong nationalistic interest. The epic hero's story deals with more than a personal destiny; his story represents the destiny of a whole nation. Historical allusions therefore abound in epics, which tend to portray the significant and formative events in the life of a nation. The "great primary epics deal with their cultures at some primitive moment of crisis."[6] Common epic motifs include kingdom, conquest, warfare, and dominion. In one way or another, epic portrays epoch-making events in the life of a nation.

The Story of a Nation

Supernatural settings, characters, and events have always been a hallmark of epic. Events in such stories occur on a cosmic stage that includes an "other" world as well as the earth. Supernatural agents enter the human world and participate in the action. This, too, is one of the means by which epics give us images of greatness and mystery.

Supernatural Element

Despite its expansiveness, an epic is tightly structured. One authority, after listing "amplitude, breadth, inclusiveness" as epic traits, goes on to say that "exuberance. . .is not enough in itself; there must be a control commensurate with the amount included."[7] Epics therefore always have a unifying hero. The action is constructed around a central epic feat, which usually consists of winning a battle and establishing a kingdom. Many epics have been structured as a quest toward a goal. Because of its sheer length and scope, an epic always has a mildly episodic plot (we can't remem-

Epic Structure

---

[4]*The Return of Eden: Five Essays on Milton's Epics* (Toronto: University of Toronto Press, 1965), 3.

[5]Hugh M. Richmond, *The Christian Revolutionary: John Milton* (Berkeley: University of California Press, 1974), 124.

[6]Richmond, 124.

[7]E. M. W. Tillyard, *The English Epic and Its Background* (London: Chatto and Windus, 1966), 6, 8.

ber the whole story at once, for example), but the wealth of detail is firmly controlled by an overall design.

The Epic of the Exodus

The most obviously epic work in the Bible is the epic of the Exodus. For literary purposes, the key narrative sections are Exodus 1–20 and 32–34; Numbers 10–14, 16–17, and 20–24; and Deuteronomy 32–34 (a retrospective interpretive framework for the whole epic, from the mouth of the epic hero himself). Several things make the story of the Exodus an epic. It meets the test of long narrative. It is nationalistic in emphasis, recording the formation of Israel as a nation and depicting the decisive events in the early history of the nation. This story, composed at a moment of national self-consciousness, was a definitive repository of the religious, moral, and political ideals of the society that produced it. The story is set in history and filled with historical allusions. It is unified partly by a normative hero and partly by the quest for the Promised Land. The world of the story is alive with supernatural intervention.

Old Testament Historical Books

If the historical chronicles of the Old Testament are to be approached as literature, epic is a fruitful rubric under which to study them. The Book of Joshua, for example, is unified by the motif of Israel's conquest of Canaan and its quest to establish itself in the Promised Land, all under the direction of Joshua. The Book of Judges lacks a unifying hero and is perhaps better viewed as a collection of separate hero stories, though certain features of the book resemble epic. The story of David is definitely an epic story. David, in fact, is the closest parallel in the Bible to the epic hero of the Western tradition: he is the warrior who conquers his enemies, the political ruler, and the representative person of his culture.

Genesis

The Book of Genesis also approximates the epic genre. It is atypical in having four patriarchs instead of a single hero as the epic protagonist. But in other respects it meets epic expectations. It is a moderately long story that traces the early ancestry of a nation. Because of the covenant theme that pervades the story, it is a story of destiny. This is much more than the history of individual heroes or even of a family; it is nothing less than the beginning of salvation history, the history of the whole human race viewed from the perspective of God's acts of redemption and judgment. And Genesis possesses to a greater degree than perhaps any other biblical story the quality of elemental human experience that epic is so adept at capturing.

The New Testament Book of Revelation is also an epic, though not exactly a typical one. It is a story of great and heightened battle conducted in part by supernatural beings using supernatural means of warfare. The setting is cosmic. The story recounts the exploits of a hero who conquers his enemies and establishes his eternal empire. There are scenes set in heaven, where decisions are made that are then enacted on earth, in a manner reminiscent of the councils of the gods in conventional epics. There are also visions of future history, another epic convention. And the style of Revelation is closer to the exalted style of conventional epic than is true of any other book in the Bible. Revelation is filled with similes, catalogs, epithets, allusions, repeated formulas, and sheer verbal and imagistic exuberance.

The Book of Revelation

Although the Pentateuch, the Book of Joshua, the story of David, and the Book of Revelation are the only full-fledged epics in the Bible, it is also apparent that the Bible as a whole is frequently epic-like. It has the "feel" of other ancient epic literature. The continuous presence of God as a character in the stories alone would make it similar to epic literature. The nationalistic tone and focus of the Old Testament lend an epic aura to the stories and even to the prophecies. The framework of epic literature, therefore, is continuously relevant to the literary study of biblical narrative, and other epics are more likely to furnish literary parallels than modern novels.

The Epic Aura of the Bible

COMEDY

When speaking of comedy as a type of story, literary critics do not mean a humorous story but rather one with a certain shape of plot. Comedy is

Comic Plots

the story of the happy ending. It is usually a U-shaped story that begins in prosperity, descends into tragedy, and rises again to end happily. The first phase of this pattern is often omitted, but the upward movement from misery to happiness is essential.

Story Elements in a Comic Plot

The main elements of such a comic plot are easy to identify. The overall progression is from problem to solution, from bondage to freedom. The plot consists of a series of obstacles that must be overcome en route to the happy ending. Often these obstacles are characters who stand in the way of happiness, but external circumstances or inner personality traits can also constitute the obstacles to fulfillment. In comic stories the protagonist is gradually assimilated into society (in contrast to tragedy, where the hero becomes progressively isolated from society). The typical ending of a comedy is a marriage, feast, reconciliation, or victory over enemies. Two contrasting ways of concluding a comic story are the conversion of villainous characters and the expulsion of such characters from the scene of festivity or triumph.

Plot Devices

The overall comic movement from bondage to freedom is accompanied by a host of familiar story elements that have become virtually synonymous with literary comedy: disguise, mistaken identity, character transformation from bad to good, surprise, miracle, providential assistance to good characters, sudden reversal of misfortune, rescue from disaster, poetic justice, the motif of lost and found, reversal of conventional expectations (as when the younger child is preferred over the older), sudden release. Whereas tragedy stresses what is inevitable, comedy is built around the unforeseeable.

Comedy as the Dominant Biblical Form

It is a commonplace of literary criticism that comedy rather than tragedy is the dominant narrative form of the Bible and the Christian gospel.[8]

------

[8]For good discussions, see the following: Frederick Buechner, *Telling the Truth: The Gospel as Tragedy, Comedy, and Fairy Tale* (New York: Harper and Row, 1977), 49–98; Nelvin Vos, *The Drama of Comedy: Victim and Victor* (Richmond: John Knox Press, 1966); Paul H. Grawe, *Comedy in Space, Time, and the Imagination*

The Bible as a whole begins with a perfect world, descends into the misery of fallen history, and ends with a new world of total happiness and victory over evil. Within this overall comic structure occur numerous smaller U-shaped stories of the type described above. Perhaps the stories of Joseph and Ruth are prototypical, but in fact such stories dominate biblical narrative. There are even stories (including the Book of Job and the four Gospels) that are often considered to be tragedies but that are actually comic in structure if we take the ending of the story into account.

TRAGEDY

Tragedy has held an honored position in literature generally. It is less pervasive in the Bible than in literature as a whole, but it is nonetheless an important biblical form.

At the level of plot or action, tragedy is the story of exceptional calamity. It portrays a movement from prosperity to catastrophe. Because it depicts a change of fortune, tragedy must be differentiated from pathos, which depicts unmitigated suffering from the very start. Tragedy focuses on what we most fear and wish to avoid facing—the destructive potential of evil.

The Story of a Fall

In tragedy the focus is on the tragic protagonist, who until modern times was a person of high social standing. Such a tragic hero, usually a king or ruler, is greater than common humanity, though not superior to the natural order and to moral criticism. The high position of a tragic hero at the beginning of the story goes beyond his or her belonging to the social elite; this exalted figure is understood to be *representative* of general humanity. Ordinarily a tragic hero possesses something that we can call greatness of spirit. All of this grandeur is brought tumbling down by a final trait of the tragic hero—a tragic flaw of character. Aristotle's word for it was *hamartia* (translated "sin" in the New Testament), a missing of the mark. Aristotle described it as

The Tragic Hero

(Chicago: Nelson-Hall, 1983), 267–99; Northrop Frye, *The Great Code* (New York: Harcourt Brace Jovanovich, 1982), 169–98.

"some great error or frailty," some "defect which is painful or destructive." In other words, tragedy always portrays *caused* suffering.

The Plot of Tragedy

The plot of tragedy focuses on human choice. The story begins with the protagonist facing a dilemma that demands a choice. Drawn in two or more directions, the tragic hero makes a tragic choice that leads inevitably to catastrophe and suffering. This means that a tragic hero is always *responsible for* the downfall (since it is the result of choice and action by the hero). Usually the tragic hero is also *deserving of* the downfall, since the choice involved some frailty of character (though in literary tragedy generally the punishment is disproportionately great compared with the fault). Often a tragic hero achieves some measure of moral perception as a result of his or her suffering.

A Definition of Tragedy

To summarize, tragic stories tend to unfold according to the following tragic pattern of action: dilemma /choice /catastrophe /suffering /perception/ death. Tragedy can be defined as a narrative form in which a protagonist of high degree and greatness of spirit undertakes an action (makes a choice) within a given tragic world and as a result inevitably falls from prosperity to a state of physical and spiritual suffering, sometimes attaining perception.

Biblical Tragedies

The prototypical biblical tragedy is the story of the Fall in Genesis 3. The great masterpiece of biblical tragedy is the story of Saul in 1 Samuel.[9] If we keep in mind that tragedy assigns a specific cause to the hero's downfall and localizes the beginning of woe at a particular point in the hero's life, the story of David as narrated in 1 and 2 Samuel adheres to a tragic pattern, since David's tragic sufferings begin with the Bathsheba/Uriah incident. The story of Samson (Judg. 13–16) is also a tragedy. Some of the parables of Jesus also enact the tragic pattern.[10]

---

[9]The best discussion of a biblical tragedy that I have seen is the analysis of the Saul story by Edwin M. Good, *Irony in the Old Testament* (Philadelphia: Westminster, 1965), 56–80.

[10]For a preliminary discussion, see Dan Otto Via, Jr., *The Parables: Their Literary and Existential Dimension* (Philadelphia: Fortress Press, 1967), especially 110–44.

In addition to these full-fledged tragedies, there are two major instances of biblical narrative where the definition of literary tragedy partly fits the story, even though the story as a whole is comic. Because tragedy deals with human suffering, the Book of Job has repeatedly been discussed in terms of literary tragedy, although the story as a whole has the U-shaped movement and happy ending of comedy. The same situation is true of the four Gospels: they conclude with the happy ending of a comic plot, but much of the action before that falls into the pattern of literary tragedy.[11]

The Book of Job and the Gospels

The most remarkable thing about the Bible and literary tragedy is that there are so few tragedies in the Bible. In a book so concerned with sin and the judgment upon sin, we might expect to find an abundance of tragedy. Yet as Northrop Frye puts it, "The Bible is not very friendly to tragic themes."[12] The Bible focuses its attention on the redemptive potential of human tragedy. While never minimizing the facts of human evil and suffering, the Bible is, however, preoccupied with *more* than what is tragic in human suffering. The result is a collection of stories of *potential* tragedy—stories on which a modern writer could base a tragedy but which in their biblical version avoid a tragic ending through the intervention of human repentance and divine forgiveness.

The Relative Absence of Tragedy in the Bible

Further Reading

Even when critics do not use the term "heroic narrative," the commonest approach to the stories of the Old Testament is some version of what I have defined under that heading. Specimens of such commentary can be found in *Images of Man and God: Old Testament Short Stories in Literary Focus,* ed. Burke O. Long (Sheffield: Almond, 1981). Explications of selected Old Testament

---

[11]On the tragic dimension of the Gospels, see especially Roger L. Cox, "Tragedy and the Gospel Narratives," *Yale Review,* 57 (1968), 545–70; and Gilbert G. Bilezikian, *The Liberated Gospel: A Comparison of the Gospel of Mark and Greek Tragedy* (Grand Rapids: Baker, 1977).

[12]*The Great Code,* 181.

stories are given in my book *The Literature of the Bible* (Grand Rapids: Zondervan, 1974) in chapters on heroic narrative (pp. 45–78), the epic of the Exodus (pp. 81–92), and biblical tragedy (pp. 95–106).

Chapter Four

The Poetry of the Bible

NEXT TO STORY, poetry is the most prevalent type of writing in the Bible. Some books of the Bible are entirely poetic in form: Psalms, Song of Solomon, Proverbs, Lamentations. Many others are mainly poetic: Job, Ecclesiastes (in which even the prose passages achieve poetic effects), Isaiah, Hosea, Joel, and numerous other prophetic books. There is *no* book in the Bible that does not require the ability to interpret poetry to some degree, because every book includes some figurative language. Even the speech of Jesus and the writing in the New Testament epistles make consistent use of concrete imagery and figures of speech.

The Prevalence of Poetry in the Bible

What, then, is poetry? We can best begin with an actual example, Psalm 1:

Psalm 1 as an Example of Poetry

¹Blessed is the man
who does not walk in the counsel of the wicked,
or stand in the way of sinners,
or sit in the seat of mockers.
²But his delight is in the law of the Lord,
and on his law he meditates day and night.
³He is like a tree planted by streams of water,
which yields its fruit in season
and whose leaf does not wither.
Whatever he does prospers.

⁴*Not so the wicked!*
    They are like chaff
    that the wind blows away.
⁵*Therefore the wicked will not stand in the*
    judgment,
        nor sinners in the assembly of the
        righteous.
⁶*For the Lord watches over the way of the*
    righteous,
        but the way of the wicked will perish.

Pattern and Design in Psalm 1

Even the external arrangement of the material strikes us as more highly patterned than expository prose. This portrait of the godly person alternates between positive and negative descriptions. The opening beatitude, strongly positive, is followed by three lines that describe this person negatively, in terms of what he does *not* do. This is followed by the positive description in verse 2. Verse 3 has a positive–negative–positive sequence. Verse 4 balances a negative construction with a positive one. Verse 5 consists of two negatives, while verse 6 culminates the whole movement with balanced positive and negative assertions.

Parallelism of Lines

The individual lines, as well as the overall movement of the poem, are also highly patterned. Virtually the entire poem falls into pairs or triplets of lines that express the same idea in different words. This is the verse form known as parallelism and is an obviously poetic way of speaking. Poetry like this is more concentrated and more artistic than prose.

A Language of Images

Psalm 1 also shows that poetry is a language of images. It puts us in touch with such tangible realities as pathway, seat, tree, water, leaf, chaff, and law court. Poets are never content with pure abstraction, though they usually include enough conceptual commentary (words such as "blessed," "the wicked," "the righteous") to allow us to know what the images mean.

Figurative Language

Psalm 1 is also figurative rather than literal much of the time. The second line speaks of walking in the counsel of the wicked. The wicked do not literally walk down a path called "The Counsel of the Wicked." They do not literally pass legislation or conduct legal seminars entitled "The Counsel of the Wicked." Nor do people literally stand together on a platform called "The Way of Sinners." People in a scoffing mood do not take turns sitting in a chair with a sign over it that reads "The Seat of Scoffers." Verse 1 is thoroughly metaphoric rather than literal.

Poetry, it is clear, uses what is commonly called poetic license. Another example occurs in verse 2, which states that the godly person meditates on God's law "day and night." There are several possible interpretations of this statement, none of them literal. No one consciously reflects on God's law twenty-four hours a day. Perhaps the statement is a hyperbole—an exaggerated way of showing how thoroughly the godly person is controlled by God's law. Perhaps, on the other hand, it is the word "meditates" that is used figuratively to mean "is influenced by" rather than "consciously thinks about." Or perhaps "day and night" is a colloquial expression meaning "in the morning and in the evening."

Poetic License

Another poetic tendency illustrated by Psalm 1 is the strategy of comparing one thing to another. The poetic imagination is adept at seeing resemblances and using one area of human experience to cast light on another area. The productiveness of a godly person is like that of a tree beside a stream. Wicked people are like the chaff blown away during the process of winnowing. The long-term, cumulative nature of a person's lifestyle is like walking step by step down a path.

Comparison as a Poetic Device

What is poetry? Psalm 1 supplies some good initial answers. Poetry is a language of images. It uses many comparisons. It is inherently fictional, stating things that are not literally true or comparing one thing to something else that it is literally not. Poetry is also more concentrated and more highly patterned than ordinary discourse. In short, poets do things with language and sentence structure that people do not ordinarily do when speaking.

SUMMARY

Poetry as a
Special
Language

From the specific example of Psalm 1 we can make some generalizations that will apply to all biblical poetry. Poetry is above all a special use of language. Poets speak a language all their own. The poetic idiom uses the resources of language in a way that ordinary prose discourse does not, at least not with the same frequency or density.

Let me say at once that parallelism, the verse form in which virtually all biblical poetry is written, is not the most essential thing that a reader needs to know about biblical poetry. Much more crucial to the reading of biblical poetry is the ability to identify and interpret the devices of poetic language.[1]

Thinking in
Images

The most basic of all poetic principles is that poets think and write in images. By "images" I simply mean words that evoke a sensory experience in our imagination. Poetry avoids the abstract as much as possible. The poets of the Bible constantly put us into a world of water and sheep and lions and rocks and arrows and grass. Virtually any passage of biblical poetry will illustrate how consistently concrete poetry is.

Reading Poetry
with
Imagination

This is yet another evidence that the Bible is a work of imagination (the image-making capacity we have). The corresponding ability that is required of readers is that they allow the images of poetry to become as real and sensory as possible. Readers of poetry need to think in images, just as poets do. Poetry is *affective* in nature, and it affects us partly through its sensory vividness.

Conveying the
Universal
Through the
Particular

Poetry offers us a series of *experiences* of whatever topic the poet is writing about. If we continually translate the images into abstractions, we distort the poem as a piece of writing and miss the fullness of its experiential meanings. It is true that the Psalms are not *about* grass and horses and rocks, but the approach of poetry to the universal or conceptual is always *through* the particular and concrete. Traditional approaches to biblical poetry have been entirely too theological and conceptual. When I read some of this commentary I frequently

---

[1]A good preliminary essay to read is C. S. Lewis, "The Language of Religion," in *Christian Reflections* (Grand Rapids: Eerdmans, 1967), 129–41.

get the impression that biblical scholars are commenting on a theological essay instead of a poem.

The first rule for reading biblical poetry, then, can be stated thus: *poetry is a language of images that the reader must experience as a series of imagined sensory situations.* The more visual we can become, the better we will function as readers of biblical poetry. In fact, our experience of biblical poetry would be revolutionized if commentaries made extensive use of pictures such as photographs and drawings.[2]

Next to the use of concrete imagery, the use of simile and metaphor is the most pervasive element of biblical poetry. The essential feature of both is comparison. A simile draws a correspondence between two things by using the explicit formula "like" or "as":

*He is like a tree planted by streams of water
   (Ps. 1:3).*

*As the deer pants for streams of water,
   so my soul pants for you, O God (Ps. 42:1).*

Metaphor adopts a bolder strategy. It omits the "like" or "as" and asserts that A *is* B: "The Lord is my shepherd" (Ps. 23:1); "their throat is an open grave" (Ps. 5:9); "men whose teeth are spears and arrows, / whose tongues sharp swords" (Ps. 57:4).

Both metaphor and simile operate on the premise of similarity between two things. When the psalmist writes that God's law "is a lamp to my feet / and a light for my path" (119:105), he is drawing a connection between the properties of light used to illuminate a pathway for walking and the moral effect of God's law on a person's behavior. When a nature poet says that God "makes the clouds his chariot" (Ps. 104:3), he intends us to see a correspondence between the swift movement of clouds across the sky and that of a chariot over a road.

Simile and Metaphor Defined

Correspondence as the Essential Element

---

[2]The best book I can recommend along these lines is Robert Short's *A Time to Be Born—A Time to Die* (New York: Harper and Row, 1973), which provides photographic commentary on the Book of Ecclesiastes.

Comparisons Require a Transfer of Meaning

Several corollaries follow from the fact that metaphor and simile are based on comparison. They both secure an effect on one level and then ask the reader to transfer that meaning to another level (in this they are like the New Testament parables). The word "metaphor" itself implies such a transfer, since it is based on the Greek words *meta*, meaning "over," and *pherein*, meaning "to carry." When the psalmist speaks of someone "who dwells in the shelter of the Most High" (91:1), the first task of the reader is to reflect on the human experience of living in a home. These domestic associations of security, safety, provision, protection, love, and belonging must then be transferred from a human, family context to the realm of faith in God.

The Indirection of Simile and Metaphor

It is also obvious that metaphor and simile work by indirection. This is what Robert Frost had in mind when he defined poetry as "saying one thing and meaning another."[3] The psalmist *says* that "the LORD God is a sun and shield" (84:11), but he *means* that God is the ultimate source of all life and provision and that God protects people from harm. The poet *says* that he lies "in the midst of lions" (Ps. 57:4), but he *means* that his enemies' slander inflicts pain and destroys him in a number of nonphysical ways.

The Twofold Nature of Simile and Metaphor

The importance of this indirection is that it disqualifies the usual tendency to talk about the theology of the Psalms as though the text were expository prose or a theological outline. Metaphor and simile are bifocal statements. We need to look first at one half of a comparison and then transfer certain meanings to the other half. The exposition of biblical poetry needs to do justice to the richness of meanings that metaphor and simile convey, and this means not quickly reducing the two-pronged statement of metaphor or simile to a single direct statement. There is an irreducible quality to metaphor and simile that we should respect, both as readers and expositors.

---

[3] "Education by Poetry," in *The Norton Reader*, ed. Arthur M. Eastman (New York: W. W. Norton, 1980), 412.

Another aspect of metaphor and simile is that they are a form of logic rather than illogic. The connection between the two halves of the comparison is a real connection. It can be validated on the basis of observation and rational analysis. When the poet asks God to "set a guard over my mouth" and "keep watch over the door of my lips" (Ps. 141:3), we need to explore by what logic care in one's speech can be compared to a soldier or prison guard watching the door of a house or prison. If the threat of death on the battlefield can be described as the rope of a strangler and the water of a flood (Ps. 18:4), we must look for a logical explanation behind the poet's assertion.

The Logic of Simile and Metaphor

This is another way of saying that metaphor and simile are rooted in reality. The two halves of the comparison are not illusory but real. In the metaphor that declares God to be "father to the fatherless" (Ps. 68:5), for example, the bond between human fathers and the character of God is real. There are qualities (e.g., love, care, provision, nurture, discipline) inherent in being a good father that are also true of God's character and acts. The poet is not simply decorating an idea that could as well be stated without the father metaphor. Nor is his attribution of the name "father" to God arbitrary. Poets do not invent comparisons but discover them. They could not *create* metaphor and simile if they tried; the relationship between the two phenomena joined in a metaphor or simile either exists in reality or does not exist. The poet's quest is to *discover* the right expressive metaphors and similes for his particular subject matter.

Simile and Metaphor Are Rooted in Reality

But metaphor and simile, though a form of logic, also go beyond abstract or mental logic. For one thing, they offer an *experience* of the topic being presented. As a result, the total meaning that is transferred from the one phenomenon to the other is partly nonverbal or extralogical. When a biblical poet pictures God's provision as God's making him "lie down in green pastures" and leading him "beside quiet waters" (Ps. 23:2), the poet taps feelings and memories within us that can never be adequately put into words. Metaphor and simile are affective as well as intellectual, experiential and

The Extralogical Meanings of Simile and Metaphor

.

intuitive as well as verbal and logical. A metaphor or simile involves "both a thinking and a seeing," as Paul Ricoeur has said.[4] This is another way of saying that the total meaning of a metaphor or simile can never be fully expressed in intellectual or propositional terms for the simple reason that it speaks to more than our intellect or reason. If a proposition adequately stated the truth the poet wishes to communicate, the metaphor or simile would be unnecessary.

The Need to Identify the Literal Reference

What interpretive obligations do metaphor and simile place on a reader? Chiefly two. The reader's first responsibility is to *identify* the literal or physical reference that forms the foundation of the comparison. That identification must be specific rather than vague, and detailed rather than superficial. This will be most evident if we consider an example that is unfamiliar to our own experience, such as that found in Psalm 16:5–6 (RSV):

> The LORD is my chosen portion and my cup;
>   thou holdest my lot.
> The lines have fallen for me in pleasant places;
>   yea, I have a goodly heritage.

The impact of this extended metaphor describing God's blessing depends on the reader's getting the literal picture first. That picture has to do with real estate, and it alludes to the allotment of land when the Israelites settled in Canaan. The individual portions were determined by lot (cf. Num. 26:56 and 36:2). The "lines" are the measuring lines of a surveyor. The metaphor, then, compares God's favor to receiving a fertile, well-situated piece of land, both for one's own use and as an inheritance to pass on to one's posterity.

The Need to Interpret the Metaphor and Simile

Having identified the literal meaning of the comparison, the reader's second task is to *interpret* what the comparison means. We must accept the poet's implied invitation to discover the meaning. In keeping with the nature of metaphor and simile, interpretation consists of discovering the nature of the similarity between the two halves of the

---

[4]"The Metaphorical Process as Cognition, Imagination, and Feeling," in *On Metaphor*, ed. Sheldon Sacks (Chicago: University of Chicago Press, 1979), 145.

comparison. More often than not, the connections are multiple. In finding the correspondences, we are exploring the logic and aptness of the comparison.

What, for example, is the logic of comparing "tongues" (meaning speech) to "sharp arrows" (Ps. 57:4)? The correspondence between slander and arrows is multiple: both are inflicted from a position of secrecy, both therefore render the victim defenseless, both destroy or injure a person, both cause pain. There is even a physical similarity between the flinch caused by an arrow and that caused by an overheard verbal attack on oneself.

We should not be afraid of the fact that the meanings transferred from one half of the comparison to the other are only partly intellectual or ideational. Some of the meanings are affective or intuitive, and some are extraverbal. We all have, for example, certain feelings about green pastures and still waters that can never be fully verbalized. Similarly, when the poet prays "May they be blotted out of the book of life / and not be listed with the righteous" (Ps. 69:28), he awakens within us fears that can never be adequately expressed in words—fears, let us say, of not having a bank deposit credited or of having our name omitted from the official list of passengers on an international flight.

Metaphor and simile place immense demands on a reader. They require far more activity than a direct propositional statement. Metaphor and simile first demand that we take the time to let the literal situation sink in. Then we must make a transfer of meaning(s) to the topic or experience the poem is about. Taking the tasks of identification and interpretation seriously would revolutionize commentary on biblical poetry. Such commentary might profitably include some photographs to enhance a reader's grasp of the literal level of the comparison.

Why do poets use so many similes and metaphors? One advantage of metaphor and simile is vividness and concreteness. They are one way of overcoming the limitations of abstraction. Metaphor and simile achieve wholeness of expression

Communicating Total Experience

Readers Must Be Active

The Advantages of Simile and Metaphor

by appealing to the full range of human experience, not simply to the rational intellect. They also possess freshness of expression and thereby overcome the cliché effect of stereotyped language. This arresting strangeness not only captures a reader's initial attention; it also makes a statement memorable. The comment that "the Bible tells me how to live" slides out of the mind as quickly as it enters, but its metaphoric counterpart, "Your word is a lamp to my feet" (Ps. 119:105), is aphoristic and unforgettable.

The Meditative Effect of Simile and Metaphor

Metaphor and simile have another built-in tendency that accords well with the purpose of the Bible: they force a reader to ponder or meditate on a statement. Simile and metaphor resist immediate assimilation. They contain a retarding element, stemming the current of ideas (and in this are very similar to Hebrew parallelism).

The prominence of simile and metaphor in biblical poetry makes the following rule the most crucial of all for reading the poetry of the Bible: *whenever you find a statement that compares one thing to another, first meditate on the literal or physical half of the comparison and then analyze how many correspondences can appropriately be drawn between that situation and the subject of the poem.*

Of course such a procedure takes time. Poetry is a meditative or reflective form. It deliberately compresses many meanings into a few words or a single picture. This is an advantage, not a liability, if only we will respect the reflective nature of poetry.

Simile and Metaphor Occur Throughout the Bible

I have taken my examples of metaphor and simile from the Psalms, but everything that I have said applies *whenever* we find a metaphor or simile. Even the most heavily theological parts of the Bible, such as the New Testament Epistles, make use of metaphor and simile, and for the same reasons that I have stated. When we read that believers are "fellow citizens with God's people and members of God's household" (Eph. 2:19), we need to identify and interpret these two metaphors in exactly the manner I have outlined. The same

rules apply when Jesus calls himself the Light of
the world or the Bread of heaven.

Image, metaphor, and simile are the backbone of
poetry. Perhaps we can add symbol to the list,
since it is often interchangeable with the others. A
symbol is a concrete image that points to or
embodies other meanings. Thus, light is a common
biblical symbol for God, goodness, truth, blessing,
etc. Milk and honey are Old Testament symbols for
material prosperity, and the throne for political
power. But in most of these instances it makes little
difference whether we call them images, metaphors, or symbols. The important thing is that we
first construct the literal picture and then attach the
right corresponding meaning(s) to them.

Image, metaphor, simile, and symbol are the
"basics" of poetry, but there are other figures of
speech that we also need to identify and interpret.
One is *allusion*. An allusion is a reference to past
literature or history. As with metaphor and simile,
we first need to *identify* the source of the allusion
and then *interpret* what aspects of that earlier
situation are relevant to the context in which the
allusion appears.

Psalm 133:1–2 provides a good example:

How good and pleasant it is
*   when brothers live together in unity!*
It is like precious oil poured on the head,
*   running down on the beard,*
running down on Aaron's beard,
*   down upon the collar of his robes.*

The fellowship the pilgrims experience en route to
Jerusalem to worship God in the temple is like oil
(simile), but not just any oil. It is specifically like
the oil of Aaron (allusion). The passage to which
this alludes is Exodus 30:22–33, where we learn
that this oil was a "sacred anointing oil" that was
used only in connection with official worship at the
tabernacle or temple. Having identified the source
of the allusion, we can interpret it: the fellowship of
the pilgrims is, like the anointing oil, a holy thing
and a preparation for worship at the temple.

Poetic Symbols

Allusion as a
Poetic Form

Identifying and
Interpreting
Allusions

Apostrophe as
a Figure of
Speech

The figure of speech known as *apostrophe* is a direct address to someone or something absent as though the person or thing were present and capable of listening. The range of things that are apostrophized in biblical poetry is too great to be neatly categorized. From the Psalms come these specimens: "Therefore, you kings, be wise; / be warned, you rulers of the earth" (2:10); "Away from me, all you who do evil" (6:8); "Lift up your heads, O you gates" (24:7); "Love the LORD, all his saints" (31:23); "Glorious things are said of you, O city of God" (87:3); "Praise the LORD, O my soul" (103:1). The supreme example is Psalm 148, which from start to finish is a catalog of apostrophes.

Why Poets Use
Apostrophe

Why do poets use so many apostrophes? Apostrophe is one of the best ways to express strong feeling in poetry. In fact, apostrophes tend to create a sense of excitement. More often than not, poets break into apostrophe suddenly and without warning, as though the statement were blurted out, breaking the bounds of decorum and interrupting the flow of thought.

Responding to
Apostrophes

How should we as readers respond to poetic apostrophes? We need to be receptive to the emotional intensity they represent. It is also a commonplace that the poet's function is to say, in effect, "Look at that," and point. Poets rarely point so directly as when they apostrophize something. Since apostrophes are often sprung on us without forewarning or preparation, as readers we must be prepared to take them in stride when they break the flow of thought. And certainly we must accept them as yet another evidence of how filled with license poetry tends to be. After all, if we heard someone in real life talking to a tree or absent person in this way we would wonder what ailed the speaker.

Personification

Apostrophe is often combined with *personification,* which consists of treating something non-human (and frequently inanimate) as though it were a human capable of acting or responding. Almost anything can become personified in biblical poetry. One of the largest categories is abstractions: "Send forth your light and your truth, / . . . let them bring me to your holy mountain" (Ps. 43:3). Elsewhere nations or tribes are treated as though they were a single person acting with a unified purpose:

Gilead stayed beyond the Jordan;
  and Dan, why did he linger by the ships?
Asher remained on the seacoast
  and stayed in his coves (Judg. 5:17).

Parts of the body are sometimes personified: "their tongue struts through the earth" (Ps. 73:9 RSV). But the largest category of personifications in the Bible consists of aspects of nature treated as if they were people: "Let the rivers clap their hands, / let the mountains sing together for joy" (Ps. 98:8).

Why do poets so readily personify inanimate things? The purposes are several. Personification makes something vivid and concrete. It is also a prime way of attributing human emotions to something nonhuman, in effect showing how the poet feels about it. Personification is a natural way of expressing excitement about something. It can also be used to show a close kinship between people and the subject of a poem, especially when that subject is nature. Finally, personification can suggest a group of people or the forces of nature acting with a unified purpose.

Why Poets Personify

What does personification demand of a reader? We first need to identify it when we encounter it. We should be responsive to the sheer vividness that personification confers on its object. We can also analyze the specific function of personification in a given passage. Mainly, though, we need to realize again that poetry is inherently fictional rather than factual. Poets are always playing the game of make-believe, imagining something that is literally nonexistent or untrue. Poetic license is the liberation of the imagination, for biblical readers as well as biblical poets.

Personification and the Reader

Hyperbole, conscious exaggeration for the sake of effect, is another figure of speech that uses obvious poetic license. It does so as a way of expressing strong feeling. Hyperbole does not pretend to be factual. Indeed, it advertises its lack of literal truth: "My tears have been my food day and night" (Ps. 42:3); "Yea, by thee I can crush a troop; / and by my God I can leap over a wall" (Ps.

Hyperbole as a Figure of Speech

18:29 RSV); "I beat [my enemies] fine as dust borne on the wind" (Ps. 18:42).

Hyperbole as Emotional Truth

How should we understand such exaggerations? We must avoid foolish attempts to press them into literal statements. Hyperbole does not express literal, factual truth. Instead it expresses emotional truth. Hyperbole is the voice of conviction. It captures the spirit of an event or inner experience. After all, when do people use hyperbole in ordinary discourse? They use it either when they feel strongly about something ("I wrote till my hand fell off") or when they are trying to be persuasive ("*Everybody* agrees that the test was unfair").

How Figures of Speech Are Alike

I have discussed the leading figures of speech individually, but we can learn a lot by also seeing what they have in common. Look closely at the following specimens of figurative language:

Metaphor: "The Lord God is a sun and shield" (Ps. 84:11).

Simile: "Your tongue . . . is like a sharpened razor" (Ps. 52:2).

Symbol: "Light is shed upon the righteous" (Ps. 97:11).

Allusion: "By the word of the Lord were the heavens made" (Ps. 33:6).

Apostrophe: "Lift up your heads, O you gates" (Ps. 24:7).

Personification: "Then all of the trees of the forest will sing for joy" (Ps. 96:12).

Hyperbole: "All night long I flood my bed with weeping" (Ps. 6:6).

Vividness and Concentration

These diverse figures of speech tend toward similar effects. They are governed by the impulse to be concrete and vivid. They are usually a way of achieving tremendous concentration, of saying much in little. They tend to be a shorthand way of suggesting a multiplicity of meanings, connotations, overtones, or associations, and as such they are a way of achieving wholeness of expression.

Comparison and Poetic License

Most of these figures of speech use the principle of comparison. They use one area of human experience to shed light on another area. In one way or another, they operate on the principle that A is like B. This is not limited to the obvious examples of metaphor and simile. With personification, for example, the object is treated as though it were a person. In using such comparisons, poets obviously resort to poetic license. They operate on the principle "it is as though . . ." instead of confining themselves to what literally exists.

We should note, finally, that all of the figures of speech cited above place similar responsibilities on a reader. First a reader must *recognize* or *identify* the figure of speech. This usually involves sensing an element of strangeness in an utterance, since figures of speech differ from our ordinary, straightforward way of speaking. Then a reader must *interpret* the figure. This usually entails drawing a connection or correspondence between two things. It always involves determining how the figure of speech is apt or suitable for what is being discussed, and what meanings are communicated by the figure. "Why *this* figure of speech *here*?" is always a good interpretive question to ask.

What Figures of Speech Require of Readers

In addition to the figures of speech discussed thus far, several others appear often enough that we should note them. *Metonymy* is the substitution of one word for another word closely associated with it. When Nathan tells David that "the sword will never depart from your house" (2 Sam. 12:10), he uses two metonymies: he means that *violence* will persist within David's *family*. *Synecdoche* occurs when a part is used to stand for the whole, as in the petition in the Lord's Prayer, "Give us today our daily bread" (Matt. 6:11). *Paradox* is a leading feature of New Testament discourse. It consists of an apparent contradiction that, upon analysis, can be seen to express a truth. Paradox always imposes on the reader the obligation to *resolve* the apparent contradiction. For example, the proverb that states "the mercy of the wicked is cruel" (Prov. 12:10 RSV) means that even the best acts of wicked people harm other creatures.

Additional Figures

Do Not Be Frightened by Technical Terminology

It would be a pity if anyone would be scared off by such technical terms as "metaphor" and "metonymy." If such terms are too unwieldy, the catchall terms "image" and "symbol" will prove adequate. The important thing is to identify something as being figurative and then explore what meanings are conveyed by it. It is also important to realize that simply pigeonholing a figure of speech with the right label is relatively useless. What matters is that we *interpret* the figures of speech and explore what meanings they communicate.

How to Know When to Interpret Figuratively

How can we know when to interpret a statement figuratively? There is only one main common-sense rule of interpretation to apply: *interpret as figurative any statement that does not make sense at a literal level in the context in which it appears.* The chief exception is simile, which is literally true but announces that it is a figure of speech by using the comparative formula "like" or "as."

Figurative Statements Do Not Make Sense at the Literal Level

We know that the statement that the wicked "clothe themselves with violence" (Ps. 73:6) is metaphoric because people do not literally wear violence. The statement that "my tears have been my food day and night" (Ps. 42:3) has to be hyperbole because it is a literal impossibility. Sometimes the context of a statement alerts us to its figurative nature. For example, the statement that "light is shed upon the righteous" (Ps. 97:11) could be literally, physically true, but the context makes it clear that this claim is made for the righteous only, not the wicked. We know that the light of the sun dawns for everyone, not just the righteous. By logical necessity, therefore, light in this context must mean God's blessing and favor, not literal, physical light.

The Portrayal of God in Human Terms

The poetic portrayal of God in the Bible represents a special category. I prefer to call it *anthropomorphism* (the portrayal of deity in human terms) and let it go at that. Such anthropomorphism sooner or later includes most of the standard figures of speech, but it is usually arbitrary to decide which term is most accurate.

Consider the statement "your right hand, O LORD, shattered the enemy" (Exod. 15:6). Exactly

what should we call this? It could be considered
metonymy, inasmuch as it was God's power over
nature, and not literally his hand, that conquered
the Egyptians. It is synecdoche if we consider that
the right hand stands for the whole being of God.
The hand could be regarded as a metaphor for
God's power, or as a symbol of that power. The
whole enterprise of labeling quickly collapses under the weight of its own complexity. The simplest
solution is to be aware that the transcendent God of
the Bible is repeatedly portrayed in earthly and
human terms and that such descriptions are of
course figurative rather than literal. The word
"anthropomorphism" seems to cover the phenomenon as adequately as any other (provided we learn
to spell it correctly!).

More than anything else, poetry means a special
idiom or language. Poetry is heightened speech
used to express intensified feeling or insight. Its
special language consists of concrete imagery and
figures of speech. These figures of speech appear in
concentrated form in the poetic parts of the Bible
and in random form in the prose sections. Whenever they appear, they require the kind of analysis I
have outlined.

SUMMARY

What, then, about the parallelism we hear so
much about? It is the verse form in which virtually
all biblical poetry is written. Strictly defined,
parallelism consists of two or more lines that use
different words to express the same or similar ideas
in similar grammatical form.

Poetic
Parallelism

The most frequently used kind of parallelism is
synonymous parallelism. It consists of expressing
similar content more than once in consecutive lines
in similar grammatical form or sentence structure:

Types of
Biblical
Parallelism

He who sits in the heavens laughs;
· *the* Lord *has them in derision (Ps. 2:4).*

*Therefore the wicked will not stand in the
    judgment,
        nor sinners in the assembly of the
            righteous (Ps. 1:5).*

Antithetic parallelism occurs when the second line states the truth of the first in a negative way or when it in some way introduces a contrast:

For the LORD *watches over the way*
  of the righteous,
  but the way of the wicked will perish
    (Ps. 1:6).

That night—let thick darkness seize it!
  let it not rejoice among the days of the year
    (Job 3:6).

In *climactic parallelism* the second line completes the first by repeating part of the first line and then adding to it:

Ascribe to the LORD, *O mighty ones,*
  ascribe to the LORD *glory and strength (Ps.*
    29:1).

In climactic parallelism the meaning of the statement is incomplete until the second line completes it.

Most scholars list a fourth type of parallelism, which they call *synthetic parallelism* ("growing parallelism"). It consists of a pair of lines that together form a complete unit and in which the second line completes or expands the thought introduced in the first line (but without repeating part of it, as climactic parallelism does):

Thou didst set the earth on its foundations,
  so that it should never be shaken (Ps. 104:5
    RSV).

He guides me in paths of righteousness
  for his name's sake (Ps. 23:3).

To call this a form of parallelism is inaccurate, since the two lines are not parallel to each other. They are simply two lines that belong together. No other identifying term has gained wide acceptance, however, and it is such a prevalent form in biblical poetry that we need some label for it. "Synthetic parallelism" should therefore be retained.

There is a caution we must remember in regard to biblical parallelism: very often it is not *whole* lines that are parallel to each other but *parts* of lines. Along with the symmetry, there is typically an element of asymmetry. For example, only the last phrase of the line "There is a river whose streams make glad the city of God" is echoed in the next line, "the holy place where the Most High dwells" (Ps. 46:4). So, too, with this verse:

God is our refuge and strength,
an ever present help in trouble (Ps. 46:1).

To make the second line exactly parallel, we would have to change it to something like "The LORD is our fortress and shield." Hebrew parallelism is not a straitjacket. It is a beautiful example of freedom within form. As someone has stated:

> It is clear that there is repetition in the parallel lines. But almost invariably something is added, and it is precisely the combination of what is repeated and what is added that makes of parallelism the artistic form that it is. This intimate relation between old and new elements is an important feature of Hebrew composition and Hebrew thought. On the one hand we observe form and pattern; on the other form and pattern are radically altered.[5]

The specific types of parallelism can be differentiated, but what they all have in common is the principle of repetition or recurrence or rhythm that is the basis of all verse forms. In English poetry this principle takes the form of rhyme and regular meter, which are lost when something is translated. The repetition of thought or content that we find in biblical parallelism survives in translations. More important than learning to pigeonhole types of parallelism is simply being receptive to the momentum and rhythm that are set up by such parallelism. The general principle is that lines are not self-contained. They belong with at least one other line. When we hear one footstep, we wait for the other foot to fall, as it were.

The Parallelism Is Often Partial

Parallelism as a Form of Recurrence

---

[5]James Muilenburg, "A Study in Hebrew Rhetoric: Repetition and Style," *Vetus Testamentum Supplements* 1 (1953): 98.

Parallelism as
Verbal Artistry

What purposes are served by such parallelism? Several, but the most important is the artistic beauty of skillfully handled language. C. S. Lewis writes:

> In reality it is a very pure example of what all pattern, and therefore all art, involves. The principle of art has been defined by someone as "the same in the other". . . . "Parallelism" is the characteristically Hebrew form of the same in the other. . . . If we have any taste for poetry we shall enjoy this feature of the Psalms.[6]

If it is not accepted simply as something artistic, Lewis adds, a reader will either be led astray "in his effort to get a different meaning out of each half of the verse or else feel that it is rather silly."[7] Poetry is an art form, an example of verbal craftsmanship. We should not press the parallelism of biblical poetry at once in a utilitarian direction. It is beautiful and delightful in itself.

Parallelism as a
Mnemonic
Device

Parallelism is also a mnemonic device (an aid to memorization, recitation, or even improvisation), as well as something that assists listening. What C. S. Lewis says about the parallelism of Jesus' sayings is equally true of biblical parallelism in general:

> We may, if we like, see in this an exclusively practical and didactic purpose; by giving to truths which are infinitely worth remembering this rhythmic and incantatory expression, He made them almost impossible to forget.[8]

We should note in this regard that the poetic parts of the Bible were originally oral literature, from the Psalms sung in worship to the oral pronouncements of the prophets, who sometimes showed prodigious feats of memory (for a notable example, see Jer. 36). Parallelism makes an utterance oratorical in the sense that its effect is particularly clear when we *hear* it.

---

[6]*Reflections on the Psalms* (New York: Harcourt, Brace and World, 1958), 3–5.

[7]Ibid., 3.

[8]Ibid., 5.

A further result of parallelism is its meditative effect. Parallelism focuses attention on a thought. It resists rapid movement away from an idea and a resultant dissipation of impact. Parallelism, writes a biblical scholar,

The Meditative
Effect of
Parallelism

> has within it a retarding element, stemming the current of ideas. The poet allows himself plenty of time. A scene, before being succeeded by another, is presented twice, in different lights. All the content is squeezed out of it. Its finest nuances are utilized.[9]

The effect of parallelism is comparable to turning a prism in the light, insuring that we will look at the colors of a statement at least twice. Needless to say, this accords perfectly with the meditative purpose of the Bible and the nature of poetic language.

Parallelism is more than an artistic bonus, though it is that, too. The words in a parallel construction enhance each other, whether through synonym or contrast or completion. It is an important part of interpretation to notice how the parallel members interact with each other, together saying more than either could say by itself.

Poetry is heightened speech. It compels attention and involvement not only through its special idiom, but also through its distinctive syntax (sentence patterns). Biblical poetry uses the highly patterned structures of parallelism in its various forms.

SUMMARY

Further Reading

G. B. Caird, *The Language and Imagery of the Bible* (Philadelphia: Westminster, 1980), is a comprehensive analysis of the resources of poetic language used by biblical writers. The most ambitious classification of figures of speech in the Bible is E. W. Bullinger's monumental *Figures of Speech Used in the Bible* (1898; reprint, Grand Rapids: Baker, 1968). I discuss the specific topic of meta-

---

[9]Gillis Gerleman, "The Song of Deborah in the Light of Stylistics," *Vetus Testamentum* 1 (1951): 176. This is an excellent source on the nature of Hebrew poetry in general.

phor in "Metaphor in the Psalms," *Christianity and Literature* 31(Spring 1982): 9–29.

Biblical parallelism has received its definitive treatment in James L. Kugel, *The Idea of Biblical Poetry: Parallelism and Its History* (New Haven: Yale University Press, 1981).

One of the best ways to understand how biblical poetry works is to contrast prose narrative and poetic treatments of the same event; Gillis Gerleman provides a model for doing so in a comparison of Judges 4 and 5, in "The Song of Deborah in the Light of Stylistics," *Vetus Testamentum* 1 (1951); 168–80.

No consideration of biblical poetry is complete without a recognition of how thoroughly poetic the statements of Jesus in the Gospels typically are; for a good introduction, see the sources excerpted under "Jesus as Poet" in *The New Testament in Literary Criticism,* ed. Leland Ryken (New York: Frederick Ungar, 1984).

Chapter Five

Types of
Biblical Poetry

To CALL SOMETHING POETRY is to identify the special idiom in which it is written. Virtually any literary genre can be written in poetry. In the Bible we find such diverse forms as poetic narrative (the Book of Job), poetic satire (much of Old Testament prophecy), and poetic discourse (parts of the Sermon on the Mount). Mainly, though, poetry implies various types of short poems, and it is the purpose of this chapter to describe the leading biblical examples.

LYRIC POETRY

What most people mean by "poem" is a lyric poem. A lyric can be defined as a short poem, often intended to be sung, that expresses the thoughts and especially the feelings of a speaker. Breaking that definition into its individual parts yields the following anatomy of lyric as a genre.

To begin, lyrics are *brief*. They express a feeling or insight at the moment of greatest intensity, and we all know that such moments cannot be prolonged indefinitely. The fact that lyrics are often sung likewise accounts for their characteristic brevity. Because of this brevity, lyrics are self-contained, even when they appear in collections like the Old Testament Book of Psalms. As part of this self-containedness, lyrics usually have a single controlling topic or theme (which may be an emotion rather than an idea). This unifying theme is stated early in the poem and exercises a formative

A Definition
of Lyric

Lyrics Are Brief

influence on the poem's development. Unless a reader identifies the unifying theme, a lyric will remain a series of fragments, and nothing can be more disastrous to the unified impact that is a hallmark of lyric.

Theme and Variation

The best means of grasping the unity of a lyric is to recognize that it is built on the principle of *theme and variation*. On the one hand, there is a unifying idea or emotion that controls the entire poem. The details by which this theme is developed are the variations. This principle places a twofold obligation on the reader: to determine the theme that covers everything in the poem, and to discover how each part contributes to that theme. Some of the Old Testament Psalms are, in fact, very miscellaneous and consist of a series of loosely related ideas. But most of them become unified wholes if a reader exercises patience and creativity in looking for a unifying theme.

Lyrics Are Personal and Subjective

A lyric is also *personal and subjective*. Lyric poets present their own thoughts and feelings directly, not through a story about characters viewed from the outside. The speaker in a lyric speaks in the first person, using the "I" or "we" pronoun. As readers we usually overhear the speaker, who may address anyone—God, himself, the stars, a group, enemies—but who rarely conveys the impression of speaking to the reader.

Lyrics Are Reflective or Emotional

Whereas stories present a series of events, a lyric presents either a sequence of ideas or a series of emotions. In other words, lyrics are either *reflective/meditative or emotional*. Emotion, especially, is often considered the differentiating element of lyric. We should not go to a lyric looking for a story; we will find only occasional snatches of narrative to explain the poet's emotion or to elaborate such feelings as praise or despair. Because lyrics are often emotional, and because even reflective lyrics tend to be mood poems, a good question to ask of a lyric poem is, "How does this poem make me feel?"

How Poets Express Emotion

It is not easy to put emotion into words, and the means of doing so are rather limited. They include use of exclamation, hyperbole, emotive words, vivid description of the stimulus for the emotion (thereby evoking a similar feeling in the reader), projecting a feeling onto external nature, or describing parallels to the speaker's situation (as when the psalmist in Psalm 102 compares his loneliness to an owl and "a bird alone on a housetop").

Lyrics are *concentrated and compressed.* They are moments of intensity, very different from a drawn-out story with highs and lows of feeling. Stories have occasional moments of epiphany (heightened insight or feeling), but lyrics *are* moments of epiphany, without the surrounding narrative context. They are intense and packed with meanings. We must therefore emphatically not expect a lyric to cover the whole territory on a given topic. Lyric captures a moment and does not give a reasoned philosophy on a subject. It would be foolish to take such statements as "whatever he does prospers" (Ps. 1:3) or "no harm will befall you" (Ps. 91:10) out of their lyric context and treat them as absolutes.

Because lyrics are heightened speech, they often contain *abrupt shifts* and lack the smooth transitions of narrative. C. S. Lewis speaks of "the emotional rather than logical connections" in lyrics.[1] Such abrupt jumps of course demand tremendous alertness and even interpretive creativity on the part of the reader.

Lyric is preeminently a poet's *response to a stimulus.* In the lyric poetry of the Bible the poets are always busy responding to something that has moved them—God, their enemies, a personal crisis, nature, victory, defeat, a beloved, and so on. One of the most helpful things to do with a lyric is to identify the exact stimulus to which the poet is responding.

The overwhelming majority of lyrics are built on the rule of *three-part structure.* They begin with a statement of theme, which is also the idea or emotion or situation to which the poet is responding. Ways of stating the theme are varied: a description (Ps. 121:1), a situation that is hinted at (Ps. 2:1), an invocation (Ps. 3:1), an address to an

Lyrics Are Concentrated

Lyrics Are Abrupt in Movement

The Voice of Response

Three-Part Structure: 1. Statement of Theme

---

[1]*Reflections on the Psalms* (New York: Harcourt, Brace and World, 1958), 3.

implied human audience (Ps. 107:1), an idea (Ps. 19:1). Regardless of how the theme is stated, it alerts the reader to what will control the entire poem.

2. Development of the Theme

The main part of any lyric is the development of the controlling theme. There are four ways of doing this, and many poems combine them:

1. *Repetition,* in which the controlling emotion or idea is simply restated in different words or images (Ps. 32:1–5).
2. The *listing or catalog* technique, in which the poet names and perhaps responds to various aspects of the theme (Ps. 23 or any of the praise psalms).
3. The principle of *association,* in which the poet branches out from the initial emotion or idea to related ones. A common pattern in the Psalms is movement from God's character to his acts, or vice versa. In Psalm 19, the poet moves from God's revelation of himself in nature to his revelation in the moral law.
4. *Contrast,* in which the poet is led to consider the opposite emotion or phenomenon as he develops the main theme (Ps. 1).

3. Resolution

In the last, brief part of a lyric, the emotion or meditation is resolved into a concluding thought, feeling, or attitude. Lyrics do not simply end; they are rounded off with a note of finality. In the Psalms this is often a brief prayer or wish.

Explicating a Lyric

The key to a good discussion or explication of a lyric is to have an orderly and discernible procedure, so a reader or listener knows what is going on. The best plan of attack is to move from the large to the small, according to the following fourfold procedure.

1. Identifying the topic, theme (what the poem says *about* the topic), underlying situation or occasion (if one is implied). This part of the explication should produce an understanding of what unifies the poem.
2. Laying out the structure of the poem, including the following considerations (using whichever ones are appropriate for a given poem): a. Identifying whether the primary control-

ling element is *expository* (a sequence of ideas or emotions), *descriptive* (of either character or scene), or *dramatic* (an address to an implied listener).

b. Dividing the poem into its topical units from beginning to end, thus showing the sequential flow of the poem.

c. Identifying underlying contrasts that organize the poem.

d. Determining whether a given unit develops the theme through repetition, catalog, association, or contrast.

e. Applying the framework of theme and variation.

3. Progressing through the poem unit by unit and analyzing the poetic "texture" (in contrast to the "structure" already discussed). This means identifying *and exploring the meanings of* the figures of speech and poetic devices discussed in the previous chapter of this book. We should isolate whatever unit lends itself to separate consideration; it might be an individual image or figure of speech, a line, a verse, or a group of verses.

4. Techniques of versification (in biblical poetry, parallelism) or patterning that make up part of the artistry and seem worthy of comment. For example, the imagery in Psalm 1 is organized around an envelope pattern in which the metaphors of the assembly and the path appear early and late, with harvest imagery occurring in the middle. After we have said all that we wish to say about the structure and meaning of a biblical lyric, there tends to remain a residue of artistic beauty that simply deserves comment and admiration.

It is by now apparent that when we speak of "a poem," we usually mean a lyric poem. In fact, most of the additional categories I am about to describe are subtypes of lyric. The further traits of each of these subtypes may provide a supplemental framework for organizing an analysis of them. But even in such cases it is necessary to make use of the lyric considerations that I have noted. A lament

Most Short Poems Are Types of Lyric

psalm or praise psalm, for example, does not bypass the general features of lyric but rather builds on them.

TYPES OF PSALMS

Let me say at the outset that biblical scholars have identified so many types of psalms, and made so many arbitrary and subtle distinctions, that the whole enterprise is in danger of collapsing under its own weight.[2] I say this because sooner or later it may be liberating to realize that we are under no obligation to use a complicated system of classification. *All* of the Psalms are lyrics, and we can do an excellent job with any psalm by using what we know about poetic language and lyric form. We should also note that classification of the Psalms rests largely on elements of content or subject matter, not on literary form as such.

Lament Psalms The largest category of psalms is the *lament psalm,* which can be either private or communal. A lament psalm consists of the following five elements, which (note well) *may appear in any order* and which *can occur more than once* in a given psalm.

1. *An invocation or introductory cry to God,* which is sometimes expanded by the addition of epithets (titles) and often already includes an element of petition.
2. *The lament or complaint:* a definition of the distress; a description of the crisis; the stimulus that accounts for the entire lament. Most lament poems are "occasional poems," arising from a particular occasion in the poet's life, which is usually hinted at in the complaint section.
3. *Petition or supplication.*
4. *Statement of confidence in God.*
5. *Vow to praise God,* or simply praise of God.

---

[2]The strengths and limitations of these classifications are well represented by the books of Claus Westermann, including the following: *The Praise of God in the Psalms,* trans. Keith R. Crim (Richmond: John Knox, 1965); and *The Psalms: Structure, Content, and Message,* trans. Ralph D. Gehrke (Minneapolis: Augsburg, 1980).

Psalms 10, 35, 38, 51, 74, and 77 are typical lament psalms.[3]

Psalm 54 (RSV) illustrates the form of the lament psalm in succinct fashion. It reverses the normal order of events by beginning with the petition or supplication:

Psalm 54 as a
Lament Psalm

Save me, O God, by thy name,
  and vindicate me by thy might.

This is followed by the cry to God to hear the prayer (the element that usually comes first):

Hear my prayer, O God;
  give ear to the words of my mouth.

The lament or complaint, as so often in the Psalms, defines the crisis in terms of threat from personal enemies:

For insolent men have risen against me,
  ruthless men seek my life;
  they do not set God before them.

The poet then asserts his confidence in God:

Behold, God is my helper;
  the LORD is the upholder of my life.
He will requite my enemies with evil;
  in thy faithfulness put an end to them.

The poet ends with a vow to praise God:

With a freewill offering I will sacrifice to thee;
  I will give thanks to thy name, O LORD, for
    it is good.
For thou hast delivered me from every trouble,
  and my eye has looked in triumph on my
    enemies.

The second major grouping of psalms is the *psalms of praise*. The English word "to praise" originally meant "to appraise; to set a price on." From this came the idea that to praise means "to commend the worth of." The psalms of praise, theocentric in emphasis, direct praise to God. Such

Praise Psalms

---

[3]They are explicated in my book *The Literature of the Bible* (Grand Rapids: Zondervan, 1974), 138–44.

poems are the voice of response to the worthiness of God.

Elements of Praise

The *elements of praise* (not to be confused with the *form* of praise psalms discussed below) are what give these poems their distinctive traits. One of these elements is the elevation and exaltation of the person being praised. A second one is the directing of the speaker's whole being away from himself or herself toward the object of praise. Psalms of praise are filled with the speaker's feelings, but we do not look at the speaker. Instead, we share his feelings as a way of experiencing the worthiness of God. In the words of C. S. Lewis, "The poet is not a man who asks me to look at *him*; he is a man who says 'look at that' and points.' "[4] Another ingredient of much praise is testimony. Praise, in other words, has a communal dimension to it, and it often occurs in a worship setting.

Declarative and Descriptive Praise

There are two main types of praise in the Psalms. *Declarative or narrative praise* extols God's activity on a particular occasion. Its main thrust is that God *has done* such and such on a specific occasion. *Descriptive praise* describes God's qualities or the acts that he does perpetually. Its thrust is that God *is* this or that, or that he habitually *does* these things. Descriptive praise, in other words, is not occasional in the way that declarative praise is. Both types can be either private or communal.

The Form of the Praise Psalm

The psalm of praise has a fixed form, just as the lament has. There are three parts.

1. *The introduction to praise* regularly consists of one or more of the following elements: (a) a call or exhortation to sing to the Lord, to praise, to exalt; (b) the naming of the person or group to whom the exhortation is directed; (c) mention of the mode of praise. Psalm 149:1–3 is an introduction possessing all three elements.
2. *Development of the praise* ordinarily begins with a motivational section or phrase in which the poet gives the reason for the call to praise. The most important part of any psalm of praise is what follows, namely, the catalog (listing) of

---

[4]E. M. W. Tillyard and C. S. Lewis, *The Personal Heresy* (London: Oxford University Press, 1939), 11.

the praiseworthy acts or qualities of God.

3. *The conclusion or resolution* of the praise ends the poem on a note of finality. It often takes the form of a brief prayer or wish.

This three-part structure is obviously a specific manifestation of the three-part lyric structure noted earlier in this chapter.

The most crucial element in a praise psalm is the catalog of praiseworthy acts or qualities of God. Accordingly, a necessary part of explicating such a poem is to divide the catalog into its topical units. Such a division will show the remarkable range in most psalms of praise. It might also uncover the presence of declarative praise and descriptive praise in the same catalog. Typical psalms of praise include Psalms 18, 30, 65, 66, 96, 97, 103, 107, 124, 136, and 139.[5]

The Catalog of Praise

Worship psalms, also known as *songs of Zion,* are an important category. They do not have a fixed form like lament and praise psalms, but they are readily identified by the presence of references to worship in Jerusalem. Many of these poems also allude to the pilgrimages that were a regular part of Old Testament religious experience (in fact, the heading "A Song of Ascents" for Psalms 120–134 shows that these pilgrim songs were sung or recited on the trips to Jerusalem). Worship psalms are among the most beautiful in the Psalter and are well represented by Psalms 27, 42–43, 48, 84, 121, 122, 125, 137.

Worship Psalms

Nature poems are also a high point of the Psalms. Although nature finds its way indirectly into dozens of psalms, there are five psalms that we can call nature poems—Psalms 8, 19, 29, 104, and 148. They all share common traits: they take some aspect of nature as their subject; they praise nature for its beauty, power, provision, and so forth; and they describe nature in evocative word-pictures that awaken our own experiences of nature. Needless to say, the poet in each of these poems does not treat nature as the highest good but allows

Nature Poems

---

[5]They are explicated in Ryken, *Literature of the Bible,* 146–64.

nature to become the occasion for praising God, the creator of nature.

SUMMARY   The psalms of lament and the psalms of praise are the two primary lyric types in the Psalter. A host of smaller categories fill out the Psalms. In addition to the categories of worship psalms and nature poems discussed above, there are descriptive-meditative poems (such as Psalm 1 on the godly person or Psalm 119 on the law of God), royal psalms that deal with the king, penitential psalms (prayers for forgiveness), and imprecatory psalms (psalms calling misfortune on one's enemies). Psalms such as 23 lack the opening call to praise of the praise psalms, but in every other way belong to that type.

LOVE LYRICS

The Bible contains some of the most beautiful love poetry in the world. It appears mainly in the Song of Solomon. The best way to understand this frequently misinterpreted book is simply to compare it with the love poetry that one can find in a standard anthology of English poetry.

Types of Love Poems in the Song of Solomon   My present purpose will be served by simply categorizing the types of love poems in the Song of Solomon. The largest category is *pastoral love poems,* in which the setting is an idealized rural world and the characters are described metaphorically as shepherds and shepherdesses. Such poetry describes in rural images and metaphors the delights of the love relationship. In the pastoral *invitation to love* the lover invites the beloved to share the life of happy, fulfilled love by metaphorically picturing that life of shared love as a walk in nature (Song of Sol. 2:10–15; 7:10–13).

A *blazon* is a love poem that praises the beauty and virtue of the beloved, usually by comparing features of the beloved to objects of nature (e.g., 2:3). In an *emblematic blazon,* the lover lists the features of the beloved and compares them to objects or emblems in nature (4:1–7; 5:10–16; 6:4–10; 7:1–9). The key to interpreting such poems is to realize that they are *symbolic* rather than pictorial; literally pictured, these comparisons are ludicrous. An *epithalamion* is a poem celebrating a wedding (Song of Sol. 2:3–5:1; and Ps. 45).[6]

ENCOMIUM

One of the most appealing of all lyric forms in the Bible is the *encomium*. An encomium is a lyric (whether in poetry or prose) that praises either an abstract quality or a general character type. The conventional formulas in an encomium are these:

1. An introduction to the topic that will be praised.
2. The distinguished and ancient ancestry of the subject.
3. The praiseworthy acts and/or attributes of the subject.
4. The indispensable or superior nature of the subject.
5. A conclusion urging the reader to emulate the subject.

Definition of an Encomium

A few biblical encomia are in prose rather than poetry, but the prose is so tightly packed with imagery and so highly patterned that it is virtually poetic in effect. Psalms 1, 15, 112, and 128 all praise the godly person (a general character type). Proverbs 31:10–31 is an acrostic poem that paints a composite portrait of the ideal wife. John 1:1–18 and Colossians 1:15–20 praise Christ with the conventional encomiastic motifs. Hebrews 11 (and 12:1–2) and 1 Corinthians 13 (and 14:1) praise the abstract qualities of faith and love respectively. The portrait of the Suffering Servant in Isaiah 52:13–53:12 is a reversal or parody of the conventional formulas.[7]

Encomia in the Bible

Further Reading

Hermann Gunkel's seminal monograph *The Psalms: A Form-Critical Introduction*, trans. Thomas M. Horner (Philadelphia: Fortress, 1967),

---

[6]For explications of the poems in the Song of Solomon, see Ryken, *Literature of the Bible*, 217–30 and 234–35.

[7]Detailed explications of these passages appear in Ryken, *Literature of the Bible*, 201–14.

remains a good brief introduction to types of Psalms. Arthur Weiser, *The Psalms: A Commentary,* trans. Herbert Hartwell (Philadelphia: Westminster, 1962), written from a liberal theological perspective, is particularly thorough on analyzing the types of Psalms.

Full explications of specimens of all the types discussed in this chapter appear in my book *The Literature of the Bible,* pp. 121–230. C. S. Lewis, *Reflections on the Psalms* (New York: Macmillan, 1958), is a thematic study of the Psalms that shows great sensitivity to the lyric and poetic form in which those themes are presented.

Chapter Six

The Proverb as a Literary Form

A PROVERB OR APHORISM (I will use the terms interchangeably) is a concise, memorable statement of truth. It is one of the dominant literary forms in the Bible and is not confined to what is called Old Testament wisdom literature. The Bible as a whole is the most aphoristic book in the world. The English poet Francis Thompson, commenting on how the Bible influenced his writing, called the Bible "a treasury of *gnomic* wisdom. I mean its richness in utterances of which one could, as it were, chew the cud. This, of course, has long been recognised, and Biblical sentences have passed into the proverbial wisdom of our country."[1]

The Bible: An Aphoristic Book

In seeking to gain an understanding of the proverb as a literary form, we can best begin by noting the characteristics of an individual proverb. I will generalize about the form on the basis of the following five specimens, deliberately chosen from diverse parts of the Bible to show how widely the form appears in the Bible.

Examples of Proverbs

1. "He who loves money will not be satisfied with money; / nor he who loves wealth, with gain" (Eccl. 5:10 RSV).
2. "The path of the righteous is like the first gleam of dawn, / shining ever brighter till the full light of day" (Prov. 4:18).

---

[1]*Literary Criticisms,* ed. Terence L. Connolly (New York: E. P. Dutton, 1948), 543.

3. "My yoke is easy and my burden is light" (Matt. 11:30).
4. "A man reaps what he sows" (Gal. 6:7).
5. "The tongue. . .is a fire, a world of evil among the parts of the body"(James 3:6).

Proverbs Are Striking and Memorable

The first thing that we notice about these specimens is that they are memorable. When we first hear or read a proverb, we obviously do not know if we will remember it, but it has a striking effect on us at once, and we recognize that it is worthy of memorization. The aim of a proverb is to make an insight permanent. A literary scholar has theorized that

> to epigrammatize an experience is to strip it down, to cut away irrelevance, to eliminate local, specific, and descriptive detail, to reduce it to and fix it in its most permanent and stable aspect, to sew it up for eternity.[2]

The proverb shares with other literary forms the desire to overcome by means of arresting strangeness the cliché effect of ordinary discourse. To create an aphorism requires a skill with language that most people lack. It is, in short, a literary gift, a way with words.

Proverbs Are Both Simple and Profound

A second excellence of proverbs is that they are both simple and profound. On the one hand, they are glorious proof that the simple can be a form of beauty. Proverbs are short and easily grasped. They strip down an experience to its essence and omit everything extraneous. Yet they can penetrate life to its most profound level, and we never get to the end of their application. For example, the observation that "he who loves money will not be satisfied with money" is a deceptively simple statement. It is actually a double comment about money: a person is unsatisfied by money because (a) the appetite for money grows by indulgence and is therefore insatiable, and (b) material things do not satisfy permanently and at the deepest level.

---

[2]Barbara Herrnstein Smith, *Poetic Closure: A Study of How Poems End* (Chicago: University of Chicago Press, 1968), 208.

Another paradoxical quality of proverbs is that they are both specific and general, both particularized and universal. Notice all the particulars in the proverbs cited above. They talk about money and path and light and yoke and sowing and reaping and fire. Yet each of these proverbs covers a whole host of similar events. Proverbs always express an observation about a general tendency in life, not about a unique occurrence. Furthermore, a specific proverb often covers a whole cluster of related experiences. The aphorism "What a person sows, that he will also reap" applies to many areas of life. Proverbs thus follow a very basic literary principle: their way of getting at the universal is through the particular.

Proverbs Are Both Specific and General

Another crucial fact about proverbs is that they are often poetic in form. Much of the wisdom literature in the Bible is expressed in the form of parallelism. But regardless of whether proverbs are in verse or prose, they frequently use the resources of figurative language. Everything that I said about the poetic idiom in the chapter on poetry applies to proverbs; indeed, proverbs could legitimately be included among the types of biblical poetry.

Proverbs Are Often Poetic in Form

Simile and metaphor are especially abundant in proverbs, as the specimens cited above demonstrate. Whole chapters in the Book of Proverbs consist of comparisons. Makers of proverbs love to use one area of human experience or external reality to cast light on another area. For example, all that is beautiful and positive about the godly life is pictured as the rising sun. The destructiveness of speech is rendered metaphorically as a fire. Jesus' great aphorism that his yoke is easy and his burden light combines metaphor and paradox. All of this means that the rules for interpreting figures of speech are a necessary part of interpreting proverbs.

Creators of proverbs are also truly literary in their ability to observe life. To write literature of any type, a person must be a sensitive observer of the human scene. This is exactly what the wisdom teachers of the Bible are. They are the photogra-

Proverbs Are Observations About Human Experience

phers of the Bible, says Robert Short in a book that is the best on the subject.[3] In Hebrew culture there were three main classes of religious leaders— priests, prophets, and wise men. Jeremiah 18:18, referring to all three, attributes a distinctive type of writing or discourse to each: law, word, and counsel respectively. There is a crucial difference between law and prophecy on the one side and proverbial wisdom on the other. Law and prophecy are God's direct word to people. The proverbs of wisdom teachers are wise human observations about reality. They rarely are direct moral commands like the Ten Commandments.

Descriptive and Prescriptive Proverbs

By placing proverbs in the context of the Bible's moral law, we can usually sense at a glance whether a given proverb is *descriptive* or *prescriptive*. Unlike moral commands, proverbs tend to state general principles to which there might be exceptions. Those who utter proverbs do not worry about possible exceptions (neither do lyric poets); they trust people to use their common sense in recognizing that a proverb need not cover every possible situation. The Hebrew mind tends to state the general rule and not to worry about exceptions (as in the claim of Ps. 1 that the godly person prospers in "whatever he does").

Proverbs Are High Points of Human Insight

Proverbs are high points of human insight. To use a literary term, a proverb is a moment of epiphany (insight, revelation). If proverbs appeared in a story or poem (as they sometimes do), we would recognize them as summing up the main thrust of the whole work. The modern story writer James Joyce once described a moment of epiphany as the point in a story where a spiritual or intellectual eye adjusts its vision to an exact focus. A proverb is just such a moment of intellectual focus. It masters a whole area of life by bringing it under the control of a verbal focus. A proverb captures the clearest and most affecting moment, the point of greatest light.

The Urge for Order

As a literary form, the proverb illustrates the human urge for order. Aphoristic thinking enables us to master the complexity of life by bringing

[3]*A Time to Be Born—A Time to Die* (New York: Harper and Row, 1973).

human experience under the control of an observation that explains and unifies many similar experiences. How many times have we not observed people whose compulsion was to make money and acquire possessions, only to find themselves dissatisfied. The insight that puts the many instances of this phenomenon into focus is the proverb, "He who loves money will not be satisfied with money." Proverbs are a way of organizing what we know to be true of life. In the words of Norman Perrin,

> The essence of a proverbial saying is that it is based on observation of how things are in the world. It is a flash of insight into the repeatable situations of life in the world, and its aphoristic form not only represents insight but compels it. . . . Naturally, in the context of a firm belief in God, the proverb comes to express insight into the way things are, or should be, in the world ordered by God and a challenge to behaviour that God will reward.[4]

It pains me to see the biblical proverb belittled as a repository of truth simply because it does not have the prescriptive all-inclusiveness of a moral command. "A maxim," Coleridge correctly said, "is a conclusion upon observation of matters of fact."[5] Proverbs are true in the same way a story or poem is true: they are true to human experience and to reality. Proverbs express truths and experiences that are continually being confirmed in our own lives or the lives of people around us. Proverbs are timeless and never go out of date. The one unanswerable proof that proverbs can be trusted to tell the truth is a long, hard look at what is going on around us in the world.

Proverbs Are True to Human Experience

This experiential truthfulness of proverbs is reinforced by the fact that the environment in which a proverb truly lives is not a collection of proverbs but the everyday situation of life where it applies. The individual proverb is a self-contained unit. Its point of contact is not with the next proverb in a collection but with the real-life situa-

Proverbs Belong to Real Life

---

[4] *The New Testament: An Introduction* (New York: Harcourt Brace Jovanovich, 1974), 296.

[5] Quoted in Elton Trueblood, *The Humor of Christ* (New York: Harper and Row, 1964), 69.

tion it illuminates. This is well illustrated by the pronouncement stories in the Gospels, where an aphorism of Jesus is recorded together with the event or encounter that prompted the saying.

The Pervasiveness of Proverbs in the Bible

Where do we find proverbs in the Bible? Everywhere. They are concentrated in the wisdom writings of the Old Testament, chiefly the books of Proverbs and Ecclesiastes. But the sayings of Jesus in the Gospels are nearly as concentrated in their use of aphorism. The New Testament Epistle of James is also largely aphoristic in form.

Indeed, the Bible is such an aphoristic book that it is hard to find individual parts of the Bible that do not contain proverbs. They appear in the brief stories of the Bible: "Am I my brother's keeper?" (Gen. 4:9). Naturally we find aphorisms throughout the poetry of the Bible: "Taste and see that the LORD is good" (Ps. 34:8). The prophets are likewise aphoristic in style: "they will run and not grow weary, / they will walk and not be faint" (Isa. 40:31). And the New Testament Epistles frequently have the memorable, chiseled effect of aphorism: "So faith, hope, love abide, these three; but the greatest of these is love" (1 Cor. 13:13 RSV). The aphoristic nature of the Bible is well attested by the large number of titles for books and works of literature that have been taken from the Bible, and by the frequency with which individual verses have been put on plaques.

An additional word needs to be said about the Old Testament wisdom books of Ecclesiastes and Proverbs. Here we find series of proverbs collected into small anthologies. How can we best read and study these books?

THE BOOK OF ECCLESIASTES

The Quest for Meaning

The Book of Ecclesiastes, the most misunderstood book in the Bible, is skillfully structured around two unifying patterns. One is the quest motif. As readers, we accompany the speaker as he recalls his quest to find meaning in life. In recounting this quest, he describes both the dead ends he pursued and the alternative to that futility, namely, a God-centered life.

The other structural principle is a dialectical system of opposites. The writer alternates between negative "under the sun" passages and positive "above the sun" passages. This dialectical principle accounts for the contradictions the book presents. When the writer describes the futility of life "under the sun" (that is, life lived by purely human or earthly standards), he is not offering his final verdict on life. In literary fashion, he is sharing his observations about how life should *not* be lived.

A Structure of Opposites

Balancing the negative sections are positive ones in which the writer portrays a God-centered alternative to life under the sun. God and spiritual values are dominant in these sections, and they transform the very aspects of life (e.g., work, eating, drinking) that are declared empty in the under-the-sun passages. It is untrue that the Book of Ecclesiastes becomes positive only at the conclusion. The affirmations made at the end have already been repeatedly asserted in positive sections of the book (such as 2:24–26; 3:10–15; 5:1–7; and 5:18–20).[6]

The Positive Passages Throughout the Book

THE BOOK OF PROVERBS

The Book of Proverbs presents more serious difficulties for a literary approach. There are some clusters of proverbs on a single topic, such as the passages on the drunkard (23:29–35), the king (25:2–7), and the sluggard (26:13–16). Chapters 1–9 are also more unified than the rest of the book. They are a coherent section of instruction unified by a common theme (wisdom), common images and characters, and a unifying plot conflict between wisdom and folly.

Beyond these sections, though, the structure is miscellaneous and the unity nonexistent. Two approaches to the collected proverbs are possible. One is a topical approach. It is relatively easy to arrange the Book of Proverbs into various topics (such as work, use of money, good and bad women, etc.). Once we have put such proverbs into

A Topical Approach

[6]For a more detailed explication of Ecclesiastes based on the framework I state here, see my book *The Literature of the Bible*, 250–58.

their topical "family," we can meditate on the complementary aspects of a single experience, much as we can turn a prism in the light to get various colors.

Reading by Chapters

The other approach is to read through a chapter as it stands. Such reading should be slow, reflective, and imaginative. This is a good way to become familiar with individual proverbs, so they will rise to our consciousness and lips when a real life situation fits a given proverb. Reading by chapters, noting the wide range of phenomena touched upon, is also true to the mixed nature of actual experience.

Reading Reflectively

Whatever approach we take, it is essential to respect the compression that is a hallmark of the proverb as a literary form. A single proverb covers a whole category of experiences. Instead of passing quickly from one proverb to the next, in the process reducing each proverb to a cliché, we need to pause at each one, making it come alive by thinking of examples or illustrations. One of the most helpful aids to a literary approach to the Old Testament books of Proverbs and Ecclesiastes is to work at finding visual commentary on each proverb.

SUMMARY

As a literary form, the proverb meets the two basic criteria of literature: it is a form of verbal art, and its content comes from close observation of life. Biblical proverbs will come alive in our imagination if we will respect the consistency with which they appeal to our own experiences in the world. To interpret individual proverbs correctly, we also need to be alert to their figurative speech and to their uncanny way of capturing the universal through the particular.

Further Reading

The best single literary treatment of the biblical proverb is Robert Short's book *A Time to Be Born—A Time to Die* (New York: Harper and Row, 1973); in addition to the photographic commentary on Ecclesiastes, it has excellent critical material. Traditional approaches by biblical scholars are well summarized in James G. Williams, *Those Who Ponder Proverbs: Aphoristic Thinking and Biblical Literature* (Sheffield: Almond, 1981), which contains full bibliographic apparatus. My book *The Literature of the Bible,* pp. 243–58, contains literary explications of Proverbs and Ecclesiastes.

For New Testament aphorism, see Robert C. Tannehill, *The Sword of His Mouth: Forceful and Imaginative Language in Synoptic Sayings* (Philadelphia: Fortress, 1975); and the works excerpted under "Proverb as a Literary Form" in *The New Testament in Literary Criticism,* ed. Leland Ryken (New York: Frederick Ungar, 1984).

Chapter Seven

The Gospels

BIBLICAL SCHOLARSHIP ON THE GOSPELS has been preoccupied with questions of historical authenticity, theological content, relation to the religious milieu of the first century church, literary precedents or models, and stages of oral transmission that can be traced backward to a primitive original from the written form in which we currently find the Gospels.

A literary approach substitutes an entirely different agenda of interests that are complementary to the traditional questions and that have been unjustifiably neglected. A literary approach begins with the conviction that the Gospels are first of all stories. Once this premise is accepted, the reader's attention focuses on a cluster of related concerns: unifying plot conflicts that move toward a final resolution; the overall structure and progression of the story; narrative and artistic patterns such as repetition, contrast, and framing; the characters who generate the action; the settings in which events occur; the point of view from which the story is told, including patterns of approval and disapproval of characters and events that the story encourages the reader to adopt; image patterns and symbolism; style (with emphasis on economy of expression, choice of concrete details that suggest a bigger picture, the prominence of dialogue and speech patterns, and the poetic bent of Jesus); and the characteristics of the narrative "world" that each Gospel builds in the reader's imagination.

The Primacy of Story

These matters have long received scattered attention, but not until recently have they been integrated into a systematic and popular approach to the Gospels. The main new factor is a growing consensus that the primary form of the Gospels is narrative or story, not sermon or saying. Above all, literary critics are now saying, the Gospels consist of characters doing certain things in a series of settings. "The genre characteristics of the gospel are. . .narrative characteristics," writes a biblical scholar as he criticizes the inadequacies of traditional approaches.[1] "The Gospel writers produced neither volumes of learned exegesis nor sermons," writes another; "rather, they told stories; and if we wish to understand what the Gospels say, we should study how stories are told."[2] And a third warns that "there are special aspects of *narrative* composition which biblical scholars will continue to ignore if there is not greater awareness of how stories are told and how they communicate."[3] In short, the starting point for understanding the Gospels is what I said about stories in chapter 2.

The Hybrid Nature of the Gospels

If we come to the Gospels with the usual narrative expectations of cause–effect plot construction, a strict beginning–middle–end framework, and the principle of single action, we will be continuously frustrated. The Gospels are too episodic and fragmented, too self-contained in their individual parts, and too thoroughly a hybrid form with interspersed nonnarrative elements to constitute this type of unified story. The Gospels are an encyclopedic or mixed form. They include elements of biography, historical chronicle, fiction (the parables), oration, sermon, dialogue (drama), proverb, poem, tragedy, and comedy.

The Realism of the Gospels

This very mixture and randomness produce an unusually powerful realism. They capture a sense both of the kind of life that Jesus actually lived and

---

[1] W. S. Vorster, "Kerygma/History and the Gospel Genre," *New Testament Studies* 19 (1983): 87–95.

[2] Robert M. Fowler, "Using Literary Criticism on the Gospels," *Christian Century,* 26 May 1982, 629.

[3] Robert C. Tannehill, "The Disciples in Mark: The Function of a Narrative Role," *Journal of Religion* 57 (1977): 387.

of what it would have been like to live through the experiences narrated in the Gospels. The kaleidoscopic variety of scenes, events, characters, dialogues, speeches, and encounters, always revolving around Jesus at the center, conveys an astonishing sense of reality.

The unifying focus of the Gospels is the central character, Jesus. How, then, is Jesus portrayed? Let us pause for a moment to analyze how three types of visual art—a photograph, a painted portrait, and an abstract painting—portray a landscape or person.[4] The photograph is virtually objective: it shows every detail as it appears to the eye (with the corresponding limitation that it cannot highlight a given aspect of the scene or offer an interpretation of the subject). A painted portrait is more selective in its details, highlighting whatever features of the subject a painter wishes to call attention to as he or she tries to capture the spirit of a scene or event or character. An abstract painting conveys only a vague impression of its subject and depends almost wholly on the subjective response of the viewer for its final content.

The Portrait of Jesus in the Gospels

Given these three possibilities, the portrayal of Jesus in the Gospels is most like the portrait. The Gospel writers did not record everything about Jesus. They were highly selective in what they included. Through a combination of selection of material, arrangement, repetition, contrasts (foils), and interpretive commentary, each Gospel writer produced a verbal portrait in which certain features of Jesus and his message are highlighted.

Because the Gospel portraits are interpretive in nature, the four Gospels are complementary. Trying to harmonize them into a single photograph is, from a literary perspective, unnecessary (though I do not thereby imply that a literary approach is sufficient by itself). Someone has proposed the helpful analogy between the Gospels and the slow-

Complementary Perspectives in the Four Gospels

---

[4]For this analogy between the visual arts and the traditional interpretations of the Jesus of the Gospels I am indebted to Robert A. Guelich, "The Gospels: Portraits of Jesus and His Ministry," *Journal of the Evangelical Theological Society* 24 (1982): 117–25.

motion replays that are familiar to us in television coverage of sports events:

> In these replays the action can be dramatically slowed down so that one is able to see much more than one was able to see in the action as it actually occurred. If one is given the full treatment—close-up, slow-action, forward-and-reverse, split-screen, the same scene from several perspectives, and with the verbal commentary and interpretation of an expert superimposed—one has a fair analogy of what the evangelists do. . . .One might add to the force of the analogy by pointing out that the true significance of certain plays can only be known after the game is over. Now they are often seen in a new light, their true meaning dependent on what subsequently transpired.[5]

As we watch a television event from various angles, we often do not even see the same people or scenic details from one perspective to the next. Might the same thing not be true of the Gospel accounts of the life of Jesus?

The Narrative World of the Gospels

Each of the Gospels creates its own narrative "world," and one of the best general approaches to the Gospels as stories is to allow them to build a total, self-contained picture in our imaginations. Someone has rightly said that in every story

> there is presented to us a special world with its own space and time, its own ideological system, and its own standards of behavior. In relation to that world, we assume (at least in our first perceptions of it) the position of an alien spectator. . . . Gradually we enter into it, becoming more familiar with its standards, accustoming ourselves to it, until we begin to perceive this world as if from within.[6]

In Matthew's Gospel, for example, we enter a Jewish world where Old Testament prophecies and religious practices are a constant force, where Jesus is repeatedly portrayed in terms of royalty, and where the teaching of Jesus is presented in

[5]Donald A. Hagner, "Interpreting the Gospels: The Landscape and the Quest," *Journal of the Evangelical Theological Society* 24 (1981): 34.

[6]Boris Uspensky, *A Poetics of Composition,* trans. V. Zavarin and S. Wittig (Berkeley: University of California Press, 1973), 137.

very orderly fashion. When we read the Gospel of
Luke, we are in quite a different world, a cosmo-
politan world in which people on the social and
religious fringes—women, outsiders, the poor,
people in shady professions—are important because they are the ones who receive God's grace.

The Gospels, taken as literary wholes, are first of
all stories. As readers we can best organize our
total impressions of them around such narrative
concerns as the characterization of the central
hero, the general (but not strict) chronological
arrangement of incidents in the life of Jesus, the
presence of unifying plot conflicts (they mainly
involve Jesus and groups of characters such as the
disciples and Pharisees), a linear or progressive
movement of the action to the climactic death and
resurrection of Jesus (if we count chapters, the four
Gospels devote anywhere from twenty-five to
thirty-eight percent of the total story to the Passion
and Resurrection), and the distinctive narrative
"world" that unifies each Gospel.

SUMMARY

If narrative provides a literary framework for a
Gospel as a whole, it is an equally good device for
dealing with individual narrative units within the
Gospels. These brief stories will yield their meanings best if we ask the usual narrative questions:
where? who? what happens? At the level of action,
these brief stories (unlike a Gospel as a whole)
follow the Aristotelian principle of one event
leading by a cause–effect link to the next event.
These stories are tightly constructed, with one
detail producing the next in a marvelously coherent
fashion. Most of them have a central conflict
moving to resolution, and many of them progress
toward a climactic epiphany (moment of revelation,
insight, understanding). The story of Jesus' meeting with the woman at the well (John 4:1–42) is a
classic case of how a Gospel story moves from one

Individual
Stories in the
Gospels

event to the next in a seamless progression from an initial situation to a final resolution or epiphany.[7]

Individual Gospel Stories as Small Dramas

Because the Gospels contain so much dialogue and encounter, it is also a helpful procedure for many of the longer episodes to lay out the story into separate dramatic scenes, as though it were a play, focusing on each segment and also noting the sequence or positioning of scenes as we move through the episode from beginning to end. Many of these stories are, in fact, dramas in miniature. As a variation on this model, we can approach some of the episodes as though we were watching the event on television. There are distant (overview) shots, close-ups, shifting of focus from one speaker to another, scenes of the crowd, and so forth.

Genres Within the Gospels

Another thing we can do with individual units within the Gospels is to identify the precise subtype to which a given unit belongs. The Gospels are made up of several general types of material. Many of them can be further subdivided (see chart on following page). There are, for example, six specific types of pronouncement stories: correction stories, objection stories, commendation stories, quest stories, test stories, and inquiry stories.[8]

How Knowing the Genre Helps a Reader

What does such a taxonomy of genres achieve? It tells us what to look for in a given Gospel passage. It usually provides the best descriptive framework for organizing a given unit. And sometimes the correct interpretation of a unit depends on identifying the precise genre of the passage. It is important for the interpretation of a pronouncement story, for example, to know that story and saying correlate with each other as stimulus and response. Frequently some of the details in a story will seem irrelevant until we place the passage into the right literary family, when suddenly every detail falls into place.

---

[7]A good model for analyzing the narrative coherence of an individual Gospel episode is the essay by James L. Resseguie, "John 9: A Literary-Critical Analysis," 295–303 in *Literary Interpretations of Biblical Narratives II*, ed. Kenneth R. R. Gros Louis (Nashville: Abingdon, 1982).

[8]For elaboration, see Robert C. Tannehill, "Introduction: The Pronouncement Story and Its Types," *Semeia* 20 (1981): 1–13.

Annunciation stories.
Nativity stories.
Infancy/boyhood stories.

} Stories appearing early in the Gospels of Matthew and Luke.

Vocation ("calling") stories (someone in the story responds to a call by Jesus to follow or believe).
Recognition stories (someone recognizes that Jesus is the Messiah or Savior).
Witness or testimony stories (either Jesus or another character testifies about who Jesus is or what He has done).

} Similar in effect, all three types focus on the Messiahship of Jesus.

Conflict or controversy stories.
Encounter stories (such as the woman at the well in John 4).
Pronouncement stories (which lead up to a memorable pronouncement by Jesus, so that both event and saying are remembered together).

} Dialogue and speech are dominant.

Miracle stories

Parables.
Discourses, sermons.
Sayings.

} Discourse material by Jesus.

Passion stories. Subtypes include arrival in Jerusalem, Passover/upper room stories, suffering in Gethsemane, arrest, trial, crucifixion, resurrection, post-resurrection appearances.

The list of subtypes reveals that, although narrative is the overriding framework for the Gospels, much of the material falls into genres covered elsewhere in this book. The sayings and discourses of Jesus need to be approached with the tools appropriate to poetry, proverb, parable, satire, and apocalypse (visionary literature).

Nonnarrative Elements in the Gospels

SUMMARY   The Gospels are stories about Jesus. To describe and interpret them, we need to apply all that we know about narrative as a literary form. Within that general category, there is much that is unique about these stories, including the range of specific literary types into which they can be divided.

Further Reading

The best overview of literary commentary on the Gospels is the excerpts collected under "Gospel as a Literary Form" and the four individual Gospels in *The New Testament in Literary Criticism,* ed. Leland Ryken (New York: Frederick Ungar, 1984). David Rhoads and Donald Michie, *Mark as Story: An Introduction to the Narrative of a Gospel* (Philadelphia: Fortress, 1982), is a model for approaching a Gospel as literary narrative. On a briefer scale, I conduct a sequential literary analysis of the Gospel of John in *The Literature of the Bible* (Grand Rapids: Zondervan, 1974), pp. 276–91. Kenneth R. R. Gros Louis does something similar with the Gospel of Mark in *Literary Interpretations of Biblical Narratives* (Nashville: Abingdon, 1974), pp. 296–329. John Drury's *Luke* (New York: Macmillan, 1973) is an example of a commentary that shows great sensitivity to the narrative qualities of the Gospel.

Chapter Eight

Parables

My discussion of the parables of jesus will focus on the ones that tell a story. Some of Jesus' brief parables are not stories but similes or analogies. To understand them we need to apply what I said about metaphor and simile in the chapter on poetry. But the longer parables are stories composed of setting, characters about whose destinies we care, and plots that move through conflict to resolution. Recent biblical scholarship has made so much of the parallels between parable and metaphor that we are in danger of missing the story element in the parables. This I take to be a great error. Furthermore, the parables, intended to be simple (though profound at the same time), have been buried under such a weight of scholarly controversy and esoteric terminology that they have ceased to communicate with power.

There is no doubt that the parables of Jesus lend themselves to almost indefinite reflection and application, but why do they capture the listener's attention in the first place? They are folk literature, originally oral. Indeed, they are the very touchstone of popular storytelling through the ages.

Virtually the first thing we notice about the parables is their everyday realism and concrete vividness. "It is 'things' that make stories go well," writes P. C. Sands of the parables; here

The Parables as Stories

Masterpieces of Popular Storytelling

Realism and Vividness

"everything. . .is concrete and vigorous. Everything is described in solid terms."[1] The parables take us right into the familiar world of planting and harvesting, traveling through the countryside, baking bread, tending sheep, or responding to an invitation. The parables thus obey the literary principle of verisimilitude ("lifelikeness"), and a perusal of commentaries always uncovers new evidence of how thoroughly rooted in real life the parables are.[2] There is no fantasy in the parables of Jesus—no talking animals or imaginary monsters, only people such as we meet during the course of a day. The parables reveal "an amazing power of observation."[3]

The Parables as "Secular" Stories

This minute realism is an important part of the meaning of Jesus' parables. On the surface, these stories are totally "secular." There are few overtly religious activities in the parables. If we approached them without their surrounding context and pretended that they were anonymous, we could not guess that they were intended for a religious purpose. An important by-product of this realism is that it undermines the "two-world" thinking in which the spiritual and earthly spheres are rigidly divided. We are given to understand that it is in everyday experience that spiritual decisions are made and that God's grace does its work.

Simplicity of Action

Combined with the delightful fidelity to actual life is the extreme simplicity of action. We can call this the principle of single action. The parables of Jesus have simple plots that focus on one main event: sowing and harvesting a crop, taking a journey and returning, hiring workers to labor in the vineyard, inviting guests to a banquet.

---

[1] *Literary Genius of the New Testament* (Oxford: Oxford University Press, 1932), 86.

[2] For a particularly outstanding example of commentary that uncovers the Oriental verisimilitude of the parables, see the books by Kenneth Ewing Bailey: *Poet and Peasant: A Literary Cultural Approach to the Parables in Luke*(Grand Rapids: Eerdmans, 1976) and *Through Peasant Eyes: More Lucan Parables* (Grand Rapids: Eerdmans, 1980).

[3] Geraint V. Jones, *The Art and Truth of the Parables* (London: S.P.C.K., 1964), 113. This is one of the best literary studies of the parables.

These simple situations gain vigor from equally uncomplicated plot conflicts. The seeds that the sower plants struggle against the destructiveness of their natural environment. The conflict between the poisonous tares and the wheat has as its background a feud between the farmer and his neighbor. The elder and younger brothers contend for their father's favor. As we read through the parables we listen to character clashes and watch robbers beat up lone travelers. There is enough plot conflict to seize an audience's attention, but probably none of the parables can be said to have a unifying plot conflict that persists all the way through the story.

Simple Plot Conflicts

The rule of suspense operates effectively in the parables. The opening situation is invariably one that arouses curiosity about its outcome. The act of sowing is a risk about whose outcome we wonder. When the younger son leaves his parental home with his share of the inheritance in his pocket, we wonder how the action will turn out. When people who work different numbers of hours get equal payment, we are curious about how the workers will respond. Often the parables turn upon a test that arouses our curiosity (e.g., the entrusted wealth in the parable of the talents or the wounded man on the highway in the parable of the good Samaritan).

Suspense

Like other popular storytellers, Jesus used obvious and heightened foils (contrasts) in his parables. The rich man and Lazarus, the Pharisee and publican, the generous employer and the selfish workers, the wise and foolish virgins are obvious examples. Sometimes a pair of characters is contrasted to a single character, as with the two faithful stewards and the lone slothful servant, or the two passersby and the compassionate Samaritan.

Heightened Foils or Contrasts

Why the heightened contrasts? Because folk stories deal with simple contrasts, because the very brevity of the parable precludes subtle shades of good and evil, and because the oral nature of the genre requires simple, heightened patterns. But the strategy also fits well with the purpose of Jesus to elicit a response from his hearers. Parables are an invitation and even a trap to move a listener or

The Functions of Contrasts

reader to take sides for or against the characters in a story. By confronting the audience with an obvious contrast, a parable by Jesus "tends to polarize the hearers. . . .The lines along which polarization takes place must be signaled by an unambiguous code in the narrative; like highway markers along the interstate, they must be legible at a glance. So we have pairs like Levite, priest/ Samaritan, laborers hired first/last, invited/uninvited, etc."[4]

Repetition

The parables make conspicuous use of the principle of repetition, which produces unity and emphasis. The owner of the vineyard goes out to the marketplace five times to hire laborers. We twice hear the prodigal's speech, "Father, I have sinned against heaven and before you; I am no longer worthy to be called your son," and the father twice explains that the prodigal "was dead, and is alive; he was lost, and is found."

Threefold Repetition

Especially noteworthy is the folktale pattern of threefold repetition, often combined with the rule of end stress (the crucial element comes at the end). Thus we get three types of soil that yield no harvest and three degrees of good harvest, three people who refuse the invitation to the banquet, three stewards to whom wealth is entrusted and three corresponding interviews when the master returns, and three passersby.

The Rule of End Stress

The rule of end stress is pervasive in the parables, leading some interpreters to claim that the last element in a parable is the most important. In the parable of the sower, the fertile soil with its abundant harvest comes last. The lesson of the parable of the workers in the vineyard turns upon those hired last. Similarly, it is the last steward who is judged harshly, the last traveler who is generous, and the last invited group who enjoy the banquet.

Universal Character Types

The characters in the parables are anonymous. Only one of them (Lazarus) is named. The result is that they become universal character types. Paradoxically, these nameless characters assume a quality of vivid familiarity, like the characters of Chaucer and Dickens. Someone has aptly com-

---

[4]Robert W. Funk, "Critical Notes," *Semeia* 1 (1974): 188.

mented that "nowhere else in the world's literature has such immortality been conferred on anonymity."[5]

The surface appeal of these stories also depends on the presence of powerful archetypes. Archetypes are recurrent images and motifs that keep appearing in literature and life and that touch us powerfully, both consciously and unconsciously. The parables are filled with archetypal situations. Jesus told parables about master and servant (employer and employee), for example, that tap our ambivalent feelings toward employers—feelings of fear, dependence, security, insecurity, gratitude, and resentment over injustice.

Archetypes

So also with the motif of lost and found that figures in several parables. All that we experienced the last time we misplaced something of crucial importance enters our experience of these parables—the panic that accompanied the discovery that we had lost it, the self-laceration and sense of worthlessness that accompanied our search for it, the relief and regained self-esteem that accompanied finding it.

Archetypes Touch Us Where We Live

Or consider the parable of the prodigal son. The prodigal is an archetypal character that represents an impulse that lies within each of us. It is the impulse away from the domestic and secure and morally governed toward the distant, the adventurous, the rebellious, the indulgence of forbidden appetites (including the sexual), the abandonment to unrestraint. The elder brother in the same parable represents something that is equally a part of our psychic and moral make-up: the voice of duty, restraint, self-control, self-righteousness. It is no accident that the prodigal is the younger son (a figure of youth with its thirst for experience and abandonment to appetite) and the other the elder son (representing a middle-aged mentality, judgmental and self-righteous). Furthermore, the parable describes a family situation, replete with sibling rivalry and parent-child relationships.

The Psychological Dimension of Archetypes

---

[5]Jones, *Parables,* 124.

The Appeal of
Archetypes

In sum, there is an abundance of human psychology and archetypal (universal) human experience in the parables. Even when the theological or moral point of the parable does not directly hinge on them, these archetypes do help to account for the powerful grip the parables have on our attention and emotions. As Amos Wilder has stated,

> Human nature has always responded to stories about quests and adventures, ups and downs, rags to riches, lost and found, reversals and surprises . . . , good and bad son or daughter, . . . masters and servants, the wise and the foolish, rewards and penalties, success and failure."[6]

Points of
Exaggeration or
Unrealism in
the Parables

I have said that the parables are realistic rather than fantastic or supernatural, but there is often an element of exaggeration or improbability in them. There are "cracks" in the realism that tease us into seeing more in them than the surface story would call for. For all their verisimilitude, the parables have an element of arresting strangeness. We think of such details as a hyperbolic hundredfold yield of grain (though not all commentators agree that this is an exaggeration), or the Samaritan's lavish generosity to an unknown victim, or the Oriental father's *running* to his son and then bestowing such unrestrained luxury on him.[7]

The Artistic
Excellence of
the Parables

My discussion thus far has focused on *how* the parables are told and has been an implied plea to relish the parables as masterpieces of popular or folk storytelling. The parables represent the beauty of simplicity, and they can be enjoyed first of all as examples of narrative art. They can be analyzed for their pleasing narrative qualities of lifelike and vivid realism, for their skill in arousing the narrative curiosity to discover what happened next and how it all turned out in the end, for their skillful conciseness in which every detail counts, for the universal character types that are part of our own life, for the archetypal patterns, for the element of strangeness that teases us (as riddles do) to discov-

---

[6]*Jesus' Parables and the War of Myths* (Philadelphia: Fortress, 1982), 92.

[7]For more examples, see Norman A. Huffman, "Atypical Features in the Parables of Jesus," *Journal of Biblical Literature* 97 (1978): 207–20.

er what the story is "getting at," and for "a structure and balance of narrative form which can scarcely be accidental."[8]

But of course we do not read the parables *only* as stories. There are several reasons why we cannot rest content with the surface level of the narrative. The stories are too simple to satisfy us at a purely narrative level. The "cracks" in the realism hint at a meaning beyond the literal. Some of the details already had symbolic meanings in Jewish analogues (e.g., sowing = teaching, seed = word, the owner of the vineyard = God). Most conclusively of all, we have Jesus' own recorded interpretations of the parables of the sower (Matt. 13:18–23) and the wheat and the tares (Matt. 13:36–43), which show that the parables have a meaning beyond the narrative level. The parable is a story that means what it says and something besides, and in the parables of Jesus that *something besides* is the more important of the two.

How, then, can we go about finding the intended meanings in a parable? My answer is much less unfashionable now than it would have been a decade or two ago: by treating the parables as allegories. I am not, to be sure, calling for a return to the arbitrary allegorizing of the Middle Ages. I have in mind the kind of allegorical interpretation that Jesus himself gave to the parables of the sower and the wheat and tares, namely, translating at least some of the details of the story into a corresponding other meaning and then deducing themes and applications on the basis of those symbols.

I am well aware that many biblical scholars have deeply ingrained objections to calling the parables allegorical. I would hope that all of my readers would give an openminded hearing to what I say in the next several pages and in the appendix. Literary scholars do not share the aversion of biblical scholars to allegory. They acknowledge only one literary classification (allegory) for stories in which a substantial number of details have a corresponding "other" meaning.

---

[8]Jones, *Parables,* 120.

A literary critic, therefore, is at once inclined to ask questions like these: Why should we deny to the parables the literary classification that we apply to the same type of literature when we encounter it outside of the Bible? What substitute literary term can possibly be invoked for stories in which numerous details stand for a corresponding person, thing, or quality? Why would we create a confusing literary situation by avoiding the term *allegory* simply because the concept is capable of abuse?

To think of the parables as being either allegorical or not allegorical is already to confuse the issue. What we find in the parables is a range of *degrees* to which the narrative details are allegorical. The idea of an allegorical continuum proposed by Northrop Frye is the most useful framework for analyzing what we actually find in the parables.[9]

According to Frye's scheme, any work of literature can be placed somewhere on an allegorical continuum. He describes that continuum thus:

> Within the boundaries of literature we find a kind of sliding scale, ranging from the most explicitly allegorical. . .at one extreme, to the most elusive, anti-explicit. . .at the other. First we meet the continuous allegories, like *The Pilgrim's Progress* . . . . Next come the poetic structures with a large and insistent doctrinal interest, in which the internal fictions are exempla, like the epics of Milton. Then we have, in the exact center, works in which the structure of imagery, however suggestive, has an implicit relation only to events and ideas, and which includes the bulk of Shakespeare. Below this, poetic imagery begins to recede from example and precept. . . .[10]

We can visualize the continuum something like the diagram on the next page. The great advantage of this model is that it does not force us into a "great divide" approach where a story is either allegorical or not allegorical. Instead, we can gauge the *degree* of allegory in a work.

---

[9]For Frye's theory of allegory, see *Anatomy of Criticism* (Princeton: Princeton University Press, 1957), 89–92.

[10]Ibid., 91.

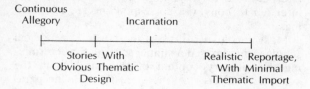

Continuous Allegory — Incarnation

Stories With Obvious Thematic Design — Realistic Reportage, With Minimal Thematic Import

The parables of Jesus range over the left half of the allegorical spectrum. In parables like those of the sower and the talents we translate virtually every detail into a corresponding meaning. Moving a notch to the right, we have the parable of the prodigal son in which, for example, the father is God and the elder brother represents the Pharisees and scribes, but in which we do not allegorize such details as the prodigal's money, the harlots, the pigs, or the shoes that the father gives to his repentant son. In the middle we can place the parable of the good Samaritan, where the story as a whole embodies the moral meaning.

But doesn't an allegorical approach to the parables run counter to what everybody learns in seminary and Bible courses? This may have been true until recently, but the anti-allegorical bias is on its way out and has, in fact, been questioned for a long time. "Certain of the parables cry out for an allegorical interpretation of their details," writes a noted biblical scholar.[11] "The parabolic narratives are never wholly free from allegory," writes another, adding that "the difference which should be emphasized is between a story which in itself is allegorical and the arbitrary allegorization of one which is not."[12] "Parable and allegory. . .are partial synonyms," writes a third biblical scholar as he dismantles Jülicher's influential theory that none of the parables is allegorical, and he, too, makes a distinction between *allegorizing* ("to impose on a story hidden meanings which the original author neither intended nor envisaged") and allegorical

Degrees of Allegory in the Parables

Decline of the Anti-Allegorical Bias in Biblical Scholarship

[11]Raymond E. Brown, "Parable and Allegory Reconsidered," *Novum Testamentum* 5 (1962): 36–45; reprinted in *New Testament Essays* (Milwaukee: Bruce, 1965), 254–64.

[12]Jones, 105–9, 137–41.

interpretation of texts in which the details were intended to convey a corresponding set of meanings.[13]

Most conclusive of all is the study of a biblical scholar who devised a simple scheme for determining the allegory content of the parables in the synoptic Gospels.[14] As he went through the parables, he listed the main details in each story and then counted how many of them have a corresponding "other" meaning (e.g., sower = evangelist, seed = word, etc.). His conclusion should settle the issue of how allegorical the parables are: the allegory content of the parables in the Gospel of Matthew is 82 percent, those in Mark 75 percent, and those in Luke 60 percent.[15]

Guidelines for Interpreting Parabolic Details

What guidelines do we have for interpreting the details in a parable? One signpost is the surrounding context in the Gospel narratives. If the narrative lead-in to the parable of the prodigal son (Luke 15:1–2) alerts us that the parable is Jesus' reply to the Pharisees' and scribes' complaint that Jesus "receives sinners and eats with them," then it is plausible to see the prodigal as a representative of "sinners," the father who forgives him as a symbol of God and Christ, and the unforgiving elder brother as a picture of the Pharisees and scribes.

Another signpost is details in the parables that had an established Hebraic (usually Old Testament) meaning: God as father or owner of a vineyard or master, seed as God's Word, sowing as teaching, and so forth. Other details rather automatically call

---

[13]G. B. Caird, *The Language and Imagery of the Bible* (Philadelphia: Westminster, 1980), 160–77. Archibald M. Hunter, *Interpreting the Parables* (Philadelphia: Westminster, 1960), 92–100, also distinguishes between arbitrary allegorizing and interpreting the intended allegorical elements in the parables.

[14]M. D. Goulder, "Characteristics of the Parables in the Several Gospels," *Journal of Theological Studies*, n.s., 19 (1968): 58–62.

[15]The easiest way to prove the allegorical nature of the parables is to compare them to the fables of Aesop. Aesop's fables *are* truly one-point, relatively nonallegorical stories, and they at once strike a reader as far different from Jesus' multifaceted parables in which numerous details call for identification and interpretation.

to mind the familiar teachings of Jesus or of New
Testament writers: the banquet or marriage feast is
a picture of salvation, the master's return after a
long journey (Matt. 25:19) suggests Christ's second coming, the father's forgiveness of the prodigal
cannot be anything other than God's forgiveness of
sinners, and the employer's payment of his workers is a judgment that calls to mind the final
judgment at the end of history.

Another long-established rule of parable interpretation that is under increasing attack is that
parables can have only one main point. This is an
extremely arbitrary rule of interpretation and one
that we do not otherwise impose on a work of
literature. It is one of the glories of literature that it
can embody a multiplicity of meanings even in so
small a unit as a metaphor. How can the metaphor
of God as father, for example, ever be reduced to a
single meaning? The one-point approach of past
biblical scholarship strikes at the very heart of a
literary approach. As one literary critic exclaims,
"No wonder there are six or eight one-point
interpretations of the Sower currently put forth,
each to the exclusion of the others!"[16]

The One-Point Rule Challenged

Even when a parable has a single *main* point,
why would we deny legitimate secondary or related
themes? The context of the parable of the prodigal
son (Luke 15:11–32) would lead us to look for the
main point in the satiric attack on the elder brother,
who stands for the Pharisees and scribes who
occasioned the parable. Is the only main theme that
the Pharisees and scribes were wrong for not
accepting repentant people into fellowship? Are
there not, rather, a number of rich themes in this
parable? Does it not give us insight into the nature
of human life as a choice for or against God, into
the nature of evil and selfishness, into the self-
destructive consequences of sin, into repentance as
the first step to true satisfaction, into the nature of
God as forgiving, into the nature of forgiveness as a
genuine personal reconciliation, and into the joy

Multiple Themes in Parables

[16]John W. Sider, "Nurturing Our Nurse: Literary Scholars and Biblical Exegesis," *Christianity and Literature* 32
(Fall, 1982): 15–21. A good source for biblical scholars to
consult.

that accompanies forgiveness? Surely we cannot ignore all of these themes simply because of an arbitrary rule that a parable can have only one main point.

Why Some Parables Have More Than One Meaning

Nor is the originally oral nature of the parables an argument against the notion that they can have multiple meanings. For one thing, biblical truth holds together as a system. In teaching a specific doctrine such as the certainty of final judgment, Jesus would naturally touch upon related doctrines that are part of the total picture, such as steward-ship or the second coming or heaven or glo-rification. Furthermore, it is entirely possible for an audience listening to a story to make continuous connections between details in the story and a corresponding symbolic meaning, provided the story is not too complex. We should remember also that a parable was not intended to yield all of its meanings at once. As Archibald Hunter states:

> the Gospel parable is not always sun-clear. . . .The Gospel parable is designed to make people think. . . .And sometimes. . .it conceals in order to reveal. Seen thus, the parable is not so much a crutch for limping intellects (as so many illustra-tions are) as a spur to spiritual perception.[17]

Liabilities of the One-Point Approach

The one-point theory is something that we would do well to discard. As A. T. Cadoux long ago noted, that approach has produced two unfortunate results:

> The judgment for which the parable asks is likely to be sought for in one element of it only and is thus unduly simplified; and all other elements of the parable are regarded as. . .unnecessary orna-ment. . . .A parable is the work of a poor artist if the picture or story is a collection of items out of which we have to pick one and discard the rest.[18]

Analogy or Comparison as the Basic Principle

If we agree that the parables are designed to convey meaning, how should we go about inter-preting what the stories mean? The basic principle of a parable is that of analogy or comparison. Literally the word "parable" means "to throw

---

[17]*Interpreting the Parables,*13–14.

[18]*The Parables of Jesus: Their Art and Use* (London: James Clarke, 1930), 51–52.

alongside." This means that the literal level of the story has a corresponding meaning, either continuously or as a whole story. Amos Wilder writes that "there is the picture-side of the parable and there is the meaning or application."[19] The corresponding activity that this requires of a reader has been stated succinctly by Cadoux: "The parable elicits a judgment in one sphere in order to transfer it to another."[20]

Once we have been alerted to the need to make such a transfer of meaning, the actual analysis of a parable falls rather naturally into a four-phase process. It begins with looking as closely as possible at the literal details of the story. Here is where we should apply all that I said about the parables as masterpieces of storytelling. If, as modern scholarship has taught us, the parables function partly as metaphors that have as a main thrust to shock our deep-level ways of thinking, then we need to let the shock at the literal level of the story sink in—shocks such as a *good* Samaritan, or outcasts being invited to a banquet while the respectable members of society are excluded, or all workers receiving a day's wage regardless of how short a time they worked.[21]

The second thing to do is determine whether any details in the story require a symbolic interpretation. In the parable of the good Samaritan, none of the details requires such an interpretation. In most parables, at least some of the details do. In either case, this is the point in one's analysis to apply the idea of the allegorical scale or continuum discussed earlier.

Having allowed the literal details to have their impact, and having interpreted the symbols, the reader next needs to determine the theme(s) of the parable. The rules for deciding what the parable is

The Fourfold Process:
1. Analysis of the Literal Story

2. Interpreting Symbolic Details

3. Determining the Theme(s)

---

[19]*Early Christian Rhetoric* (Cambridge: Harvard University Press, 1971), 74.

[20]*The Parables of Jesus*, 56.

[21]Good discussions of the parables as an assault on the reader's "deep structures" of thinking include Robert W. Funk, *Language, Hermeneutic and the Word of God* (New York: Harper and Row, 1966); John Dominic Crossan, *The Dark Interval* (Niles, Ill.: Argus, 1975); Sallie TeSelle, *Speaking in Parables* (Philadelphia: Fortress, 1975).

about are exactly the same as those for stories in general (see pages 33–73). Often the surrounding context in the Gospels already establishes an interpretive framework, but even in such instances the parable might have implicit themes beyond the one(s) suggested by the lead-in or concluding comment. In the parable of the talents, once we have interpreted the allegory (the master = God or Christ; the entrusted money = abilities, time, and opportunities; the master's commendation and condemnation = the final judgment; and so forth), we then have to decide what *themes* are conveyed by this mixture of narrative and allegory. Using what we know about the doctrines of the Bible and the clues that are inherent in the very nature of this parable's action, it is easy to interpret the parable as embodying ideas about stewardship or calling, the sovereignty of God as creator and judge, and the eschatological doctrines of the second coming and heaven/hell as the destination of people.

4. Application

Having identified the theme(s), there is, fourth, the matter of application. Granted that themes *a*, *b*, and *c* are present in a given parable, to whom, or how, did those themes apply in the specific context in which Jesus uttered them? And furthermore, how do those same themes apply today? As with other parts of the Bible, interpretation deals with the double question of what a parable meant *then* and what it means *now*. [22]

SUMMARY

The parables of Jesus are masterpieces of story-telling. We should first of all enjoy them in the same ways that we enjoy other stories. These simple stories are didactic in their purpose. Before they fully interest us or assume their true significance, we must usually attach a symbolic meaning to some of the details in the story, and we must always find one or more religious themes in them.

---

[22]For a good statement of the literary principle that we need to see universal as well as first-century meanings in the parables, see Jones, "Toward a Wider Interpretation," 135–66 in *The Art and Truth of the Parables*. A lot of modern parable scholarship has surrounded the parables with so much first-century context that it becomes hard to see their relevance for twentieth-century people.

Further Reading

The most convenient starting point is the excerpts collected under "Parable" in *The New Testament in Literary Criticism,* ed. Leland Ryken (New York: Frederick Ungar, 1984). The sources cited in the foregoing footnotes are all profitable ones to consult. Much of the scholarship on the parables that has been touted as being a literary approach strikes me as the worst possible type of pedantry.

Chapter Nine

The Epistles

THE EPISTLE IS THE DOMINANT LITERARY GENRE of the New Testament in terms of space. It is a mixed form that combines literary and expository features. The New Testament Epistles are, moreover, a combination of private correspondence and public address. They may lean in a literary or nonliterary direction, depending on how a given writer on a given occasion treats the letter form. At no point, however, can we understand the New Testament Epistles without applying literary principles.

A Mixed Form

The New Testament epistle has a relatively fixed form, consisting of five main parts:

Epistolary Structure

1. Opening or salutation (sender, addressee, greeting).
2. Thanksgiving (including such features as prayer for spiritual welfare, remembrance of the recipient[s], and eschatological climax).
3. Body of the letter (beginning with introductory formulae and concluding with eschatological and travel material).
4. Paraenesis (moral exhortations).
5. Closing (final greetings and benediction).

This formal element in the New Testament Epistles satisfies the literary impulse for pattern and design, and it proves that the writers self-consciously met certain understood conventions of letter writing when they wrote the Epistles.

Discerning the Unity of an Epistle

The letter form requires different activities from a reader than stories and poems do. One thing all of these forms *do* have in common is that they will yield most if they are read as literary *wholes,* preferably in a single sitting. But the flow of a letter is topical and logical, in contrast to the flow of events that makes up a story or the sequence of feelings in a lyric poem. The best way of outlining an epistle is by topics, noting how one argument leads logically to the next. The most crucial rule of all is to "think paragraphs" when reading an epistle.[1]

The Real-Life Situations in the Epistles

Despite the expository and logical nature of the writing in the Epistles, they nonetheless possess the experiential immediacy that we expect of literature. The Epistles are not essays in systematic theology which the apostles sat down to compose in their studies. They are letters addressed to specific people and situations. They convey a sense of actual life in the manner of other literature. Taken together, the New Testament Epistles yield a vivid picture of the varied life of the early Christian church.

Their Occasional Nature

Because they arise from specific occasions, the Epistles should not be pressed into a more systematic form than they are intended to have. As one biblical scholar has stated,

> Since these are letters, the points argued and stressed are often not those of the greatest importance. They are usually points about which differences of opinion existed. . . .The churches addressed. . .knew [the author's] views on the great central facts; these he can take for granted. It is to show them their mistakes in the application of these central facts to their daily life, to help their doubts, that he writes. . . .Many of the questions he discusses are those propounded by the perplexed church. He answers the question because it has been raised.[2]

---

[1]This advice comes from Gordon Fee and Douglas Stuart, *How to Read the Bible for All Its Worth* (Grand Rapids: Zondervan, 1982), 51.

[2]Morton Scott Enslin, *The Literature of the Christian Movement* (New York: Harper and Row, 1938, 1956), 214.

In a word, the Epistles are *occasional* letters evoked by a specific situation, not formal essays on theological topics.

One of the literary features of the Epistles is the specific genres that are embedded in them. Proverbs and aphoristic sayings abound ("Bad company corrupts good character," 1 Cor. 15:33; "a little yeast works through the whole batch of dough," Gal. 5:9). There are liturgical formulas, creedal affirmations, and hymns (e.g., Gal. 5:14; Phil. 2:6–11; Col. 1:15–20; 1 Tim. 3:16). Lists of vices and virtues are also a recognizable form (e.g., Rom. 1:29–31; Gal. 5:22–23), as is the imperative cluster (e.g., Col. 3).

Literary Genres Within the Epistles

Another thing that makes the Epistles literary is their reliance on the resources of poetic language and figures of speech. Metaphor and simile are common: *"gluing* yourselves to the good"; *"boiling* with the spirit"; "let the love of Christ *make its home in you";* "let the peace of Christ be *umpire* in your hearts."[3] Many of the comparisons are extended ones that ask for detailed analysis (such as the complete armor of the Christian in Eph. 6:10–17). Other rhetorical and poetic devices require more of a willingness to be receptive to their affective style. I refer to such forms as *rhetorical questions* ("If God is for us, who is against us?"), *paradox* ("when I am weak, then I am strong"), *questions and exclamations* ("What then shall we say? That the law is sin? By no means!"), and *apostrophe* ("O death, where is thy sting?").

Poetic Language

Yet another literary element in the Epistles is their rhetoric and style. To experience the full impact of these letters requires us to be sensitive to the masterful use of repetition, balance, antithesis, and parallel constructions. All of them are present on a small scale in the following passage (2 Cor. 4:8–9):

Rhetorical Patterns

> We are hard pressed on every side,
>   but not crushed;
> perplexed, but not in despair;

---

[3] I have taken these translations from P. C. Sands, *Literary Genius of the New Testament* (Oxford: Oxford University Press, 1932), 153.

persecuted, but not abandoned;
struck down, but not destroyed.

The same rhetorical features appear on a much grander scale elsewhere, and in an instance such as 1 Corinthians 13 the elaborate patterning becomes an example of great art.

SUMMARY   The forcefulness, beauty, and affective power of the New Testament Epistles are not accidental. They are the product of artistic and highly patterned prose. The New Testament Epistles employ a fixed form, incorporate smaller literary genres into the overriding letter form, and rely on poetic language and stylistic patterns to communicate their meanings with power. The corresponding skills that they require from readers are the ability *to determine the overall structure of an epistle, to "think paragraphs" in following the logical flow of ideas, to interpret figurative language, and to be sensitive to the effects of artistic patterning.*

Further Reading

A wealth of literary criticism on the Epistles has been collected in *The New Testament in Literary Criticism,* ed. Leland Ryken (New York: Frederick Ungar, 1984), in sections on "Epistle" and "Paul as Letter Writer." For stylistic analysis of rhetorical patterns, see P. C. Sands, *Literary Genius of the New Testament* (Oxford: Oxford University Press, 1932), pp. 128–84; and Ryken, *The Literature of the Bible,* pp. 317–31. Good general studies include Calvin J. Roetzel, *The Letters of Paul: Conversations in Context* (Atlanta: John Knox, 1975), and William G. Doty, *Letters in Primitive Christianity* (Philadelphia: Fortress, 1973).

Chapter Ten

Satire

THERE IS MORE SATIRE IN THE BIBLE than one would guess from standard discussions. Many a passage in the Bible would make a great deal more sense to us if we simply added satire to our lexicon of literary terms.

Satire is the exposure, through ridicule or rebuke, of human vice or folly. An object of attack is the essential ingredient. Thus defined, satire is not inherently literary, since the exposure of vice or folly can occur in nonliterary as well as literary writing. Satire becomes literary when the controlling purpose of attack is combined with a literary method, such as fiction, story, description of characters, metaphor, and so forth. Satire may appear in any literary genre (such as narrative, lyric, or parable), and it may be either a minor part of a work or the main content of an entire work. Although satire usually has one main object of attack, satiric works often make a number of jabs in various directions, a feature that has been called "satiric ripples."

In any literary satire, there are four main elements that require the reader's attention. The first is the object(s) of attack. The object of attack might be a single thing. Thus the parable of the rich man and Lazarus (Luke 16:19–31) attacks love of money and the callous unconcern that it encourages, and the Book of Jonah exposes the type of Jewish ethnocentrism that tried to make God's mercy the exclusive property of the Jews. But in a satire such as the Book of Amos or Jesus' satiric discourse against the Pharisees in Matthew 23, the list of things being attacked is an ever-expanding list of diverse abuses. Another thing to note about the object of attack is that it can be either a historical particular or a universal vice. The parable of the Pharisee and the tax collector (Luke 18:9–14), for example, is specifically an attack on the self-righteousness of the Pharisees, while the parable of the rich fool (Luke 12:13–21) is not about a specific category of materialistic people but about covetous greed in general.

The Satiric Vehicle

The second thing to note in a satire is the satiric vehicle. Story is one of the commonest satiric vehicles, as in the story of Jonah or the satiric parables of Jesus. In the absence of a full-fledged story, there can be brief snatches of action, as when Amos recounts the immoral actions of which Israel is guilty (Amos 2:6–12), or when Isaiah briefly narrates how idol worshipers first have a goldsmith make an image and then fall down before the lifeless statue (Isa. 46:5–7). The portrait technique or character sketch is a standard form with satirists. Typical specimens are Ezekiel's satiric portrait of the prince of Tyre (Ezek. 28:1–19) or Isaiah's portrait of the haughty women of Jerusalem, who can be seen

walking along with outstretched necks,
   flirting with their eyes,
tripping along with mincing steps,
   with ornaments jingling on their ankles (Isa.
      3:16).

Such literary forms as narrative and portrait are among the more artistic and sophisticated types of satiric vehicle. At the more informal end of the spectrum we find an array of cruder satiric weapons. One is direct vituperation or denunciation: "Hear this word, you cows of Bashan. . . ," shouts Amos to the wealthy women of Israel (4:1). The "woe formula" is equally direct: "Woe to you, scribes and Pharisees. . . ," Jesus repeatedly says in Matthew 23. A satiric vehicle can be as brief and simple as a derogatory epithet or title ("you blind guides," Jesus calls the Pharisees in Matt. 23:16,

23), or an uncomplimentary metaphor or simile, as when Jesus compares the Pharisees to whitewashed tombs that are outwardly beautiful but inwardly filled with repulsive decay (Matt. 23:27–28).

Thirdly, satire always has a prevailing tone. There are two possibilities, which literary scholars have named after two Roman satirists. Horatian satire is gently urbane, smiling, subtle. It aims to correct folly or vice by gentle laughter, on the premise that it can be laughed out of existence. Examples of the "soft sell" approach to satire include the story of Jonah, the pouting prophet; Isaiah's rollicking story of the steps by which a pagan fashions an idol out of wood and uses part of the very same piece of wood to build a fire (Isa. 44:9–17); and Jesus' hilarious portrait of the Pharisees who "strain out a gnat but swallow a camel" (Matt. 23:24).

The Satiric Tone

The other type of satire, traditionally known as Juvenalian satire, is biting, bitter, and angry in tone. It does not try to laugh vice out of existence but instead attempts to lash it out of existence. It points with contempt and moral indignation at the corruptness and evil of people and institutions. Most satire in the Bible is of this type, and it includes a large quantity of scorn (as distinct from humorous laughter).

Finally, satire always has a stated or implied satiric norm—a standard by which the object of attack is being criticized. The satiric norm is the positive model that is offered to the reader as an alternative to the negative picture that always dominates a satiric work. In the story of Jonah, for example, the universal mercy of God extended to the repentant city of Nineveh is a positive foil to the misguided nationalism of Jonah. In the Sermon on the Mount, each of Jesus' satiric charges against the Pharisees is accompanied by a positive command (Matt. 6:1–14).

The Satiric Norm

Where can we find this type of satire in the Bible? Virtually everywhere. Books such as Jonah and Amos are wholly satiric. Other books are heavily satiric; for example, the Book of Job holds up the orthodox "comforters" to rebuke, and the

The Pervasiveness of Satire in the Bible

Book of Ecclesiastes is a prolonged satiric attack against a society that is much like our own—acquisitive, materialistic, hedonistic, secular. Many of Jesus' parables are satiric (e.g., the rich man and Lazarus, and the Pharisee and the publican). There is a satiric thread in biblical narrative whenever a character's flaws are prominently displayed (for example, Jacob's greed, Haman's pride, and the Pharisees' antagonism to Jesus in the Gospels). Satire can show up in lyric poetry, as in taunt songs directed against the worshipers of idols, or the portraits of the speaker's enemies in the psalms of lament. Many biblical proverbs have a satiric edge ("Like a gold ring in a pig's snout is a beautiful woman who shows no discretion," Prov. 11:22). And the discourses of Jesus in the Gospels are often satiric.

Satire in
Biblical
Prophecy

The largest category of satire in the Bible is prophetic writing. The two major types of prophetic oracle (pronouncement) are the oracle of judgment and the oracle of salvation. The best literary approach to the oracle of judgment is satire. These passages always have a discernible object of attack, a standard by which the judgment is rendered, and a vehicle of attack (at its simplest, it consists of a prediction of calamity in which the prophet pictures in vivid and specific detail a reversal of present conditions). Such satiric oracles of judgment pervade the prophetic books of the Bible; typical specimens are Isaiah 5; Ezekiel 28:1–19; and Ezekiel 34.

SUMMARY

Much of the Bible's truth and wisdom have been enshrined in the form of satire. By framing truth as an attack on vice or folly, biblical satire drives its point home with an electric charge. Usually the attack is conducted by means of a discernible literary technique. Despite the negative approach of the satirist (who is always busy attacking someone or something), a positive norm emerges from biblical satire because it includes a foil to the evil that is attacked. That foil is usually the character or law of God. Satire is an unsettling genre. Its aim is to induce discomfort with the way things are, which explains why there is so much of it in the Bible. The reader's task with satire is fourfold: to *identify the object(s) of attack, the satiric vehicle, the tone, and the norm or standard by which things are criticized.*

Further Reading

Leland Ryken, *The Literature of the Bible* (Grand Rapids: Zondervan, 1974), pp. 261–70; Edwin M. Good, *Irony in the Old Testament* (Philadelphia: Westminster, 1965), as indicated in the index; Harry Boonstra, "Satire in Matthew," *Christianity and Literature,* 29, no. 4 (Summer 1980): 32–45; Elton Trueblood, *The Humor of Christ* (New York: Harper and Row, 1964), especially chapter 4. Although it does not use the framework of literary satire, Claus Westermann's *Basic Forms of Prophetic Speech,* trans. Hugh C. White (Philadelphia: Westminster, 1967), has material that can easily be assimilated into the category of satire.

Chapter Eleven

Visionary Literature

THE CONTENT OF LITERATURE AS A WHOLE falls into two large categories. Some literature presents a replica of existing reality; the usual term for such literature is realism. Other literature presents an alternative to known reality. It does not imitate empirical reality but creates or imagines an alternate reality. The standard term for such literature is fantasy.

The Two Types of Literature

The Bible's tendency toward realism is a commonplace. Its staple is historical narrative and biography. Even the fictional parables of Jesus stay close to the way things are in everyday reality.

But the other type of literature is also well-represented, chiefly in the related genres of prophecy and apocalypse. I have decided to discuss this amorphous body of literature under the single heading of visionary literature. Visionary literature pictures settings, characters, and events that differ from ordinary reality. This is not to say that the things described in visionary literature did not happen in past history or will not happen in future history. But it does mean that the things as pictured by the writer at the time of writing exist in the imagination, not in empirical reality.

Visionary Literature Defined

In discussing prophecy and apocalypse together I do not mean to imply that these biblical forms do not have distinguishing traits that make them different from each other. Nor am I saying that they are *wholly* visionary. Prophecy, especially, contains much that is straightforward preaching

Prophecy and Apocalypse Are Partly Visionary

and prediction, and many of its judgments can best be approached under the literary category of satire.

Still, the visionary element is strong in both genres, and my purpose is to delineate the rhetoric and literary forms that will allow a reader to make literary sense of these writings. They are among the most literary parts of the Bible but are so different from familiar types of literature that they often get bypassed in literary discussions. By discussing them under this visionary aspect, I am obviously omitting much that could be said about both genres. I should also note that the visionary element in such literature should by no means be regarded as necessarily futuristic in orientation.

The Element of Otherness

I have already hinted at the first thing we should notice about visionary literature: the element of otherness. Visionary literature transforms the known world or the present state of things into a situation that at the time of writing is as yet only imagined. In one way or another, visionary literature takes us to a strange world where ordinary rules of reality no longer prevail.

Reversal and Transformation as Visionary Themes

The simplest form of such transformation is a futuristic picture of the changed fortunes of a person or group or nation. In the prophetic oracle of judgment, for example, the currently powerful individual or group is pictured as defeated, contrary to all that is apparent at the time of writing:

You women who are so complacent,
  rise up and listen to me;
you daughters who feel secure,
  hear what I have to say!
In little more than a year
  you who feel secure will tremble;
the grape harvest will fail,
  and the harvest of fruit will not come. . . .
The fortress will be abandoned,
  the noisy city deserted;
citadel and watchtower will become a
    wasteland forever,
    the delight of donkeys, a pasture for flocks
                    (Isa. 32:9–10, 14).

In the oracle of redemption, this pattern is reversed. Instead of a coming woe more terrible than anything that presently exists, those to whom the oracle is addressed will receive a blessing that is the opposite of anything they currently experience:

> *"The days are coming," declares the LORD,*
>   *"when the reaper will be overtaken by the*
>   *plowman*
>   *and the planter by the one treading grapes.*
> *New wine will drip from the mountains*
>   *and flow from all the hills"*
>
> *(Amos 9:13).*

The motifs of transformation and reversal are prominent in visionary literature, and they lead to this principle of interpretation: *in visionary literature, be ready for the reversal of ordinary reality.*

The otherness of visionary writing is often more radical than the temporal reversals and changing fortunes just noted. A leading element of visionary literature is the portrayal of a transcendental or supernatural world. In the Bible this other world is usually heaven, but there are also visions of hell. Visions of either type do not primarily take the reader forward in time but rather beyond the visible spatial world. One thinks at once of such passages as Isaiah's vision of God sitting on his heavenly throne (6:1–5), or Ezekiel's vision of the divine chariot (Ezek. 1), or scenes of heavenly worship in the Book of Revelation (e.g., ch. 4), or the description of the New Jerusalem in the last two chapters of Revelation. The element of transcendence is pervasive in visionary literature, and it, too, can be formulated as a principle: *when reading visionary literature, be prepared to use your imagination to picture a world that transcends earthly reality.* Visionary literature assaults a purely mundane mindset; in fact, this is one of its main purposes.

Transcendental Realms as a Visionary Theme

The strangeness in visionary literature extends to both scenes and actors. The scene is cosmic, not localized. In Old Testament prophecy it extends to whole nations. In apocalyptic works it encompasses the entire earth and reaches beyond it to heaven and hell. In the Book of Revelation, for example, we move in a regular rhythm between

The Cosmic Scope of Visionary Literature

heaven and earth, and the scenes set on earth involve the entire planet. The action, moreover, eventually reaches out to include the whole human race throughout all of history. Old Testament prophecy is similar; Richard Moulton writes:

> These prophetic dramas are such as no theatre could compass. For their state they need all space; and the time of their action extends to the end of all things. The speakers include God and the Celestial Hosts; Israel appears, Israel Suffering and Israel Repentant; Sinners in Zion, the Godly in Zion; the Saved and the Doomed, the East and West, answer one another.[1]

Supernatural Agents and Strange Creatures

Filling this cosmic stage are actors that do not fit ordinary expectations. God and angels and glorified saints in heaven seem appropriate enough in the heavenly scenes, and they are leading actors in the visionary literature of the Bible. But other creatures are more startling to earthly eyes: a great red dragon (Rev. 12:3–4), "living creatures" with "six wings and. . .covered with eyes all around" (Rev. 4:8), a warrior riding a red horse (Rev. 6:4), two flying women with wings like those of a stork (Zech. 5:9), or a beast that "was like a lion, and it had the wings of an eagle," which had its wings plucked off and then stood "on two feet like a man" (Dan. 7:4).

Inanimate Forces as Actors

Such mingling of the familiar and unfamiliar, a hallmark of visionary literature, takes an even stranger form when inanimate objects and forces of nature suddenly become actors, as in this vision of imminent military invasion in Isaiah 13:10:

The stars of heaven and their constellations
will not show their light.
The rising sun will be darkened
and the moon will not give its light.

Such breaking down of ordinary distinctions between the human and the natural realms is equally pervasive in the Book of Revelation:

> The woman was given the wings of a great eagle, so that she might fly to the place prepared for her in

---

[1]*The Modern Reader's Bible* (New York: Macmillan, 1895, 1935), 1392.

the desert. . . .Then from his mouth the serpent spewed forth water like a river, to overtake the woman and sweep her away with the torrent. But the earth helped the woman by opening its mouth and swallowing the river that the dragon had spewed out of his mouth (Rev. 12:14–16). .

In the strange and frequently surrealistic world of visionary literature, virtually any aspect of creation can become a participant in the ongoing drama of God's judgments and redemption. It is a world where a river can overflow a nation (Isa. 8:5–8), where a branch can build a temple (Zech. 6:12) and a ram's horn can grow to the sky and knock stars to the ground (Dan. 8:9–10). Sea, clouds, earthquake, storm, whirlwind, and assorted animals are constant actors in visionary literature. This is obviously a type of fantasy literature, not because the events symbolically portrayed are unreal or untrue, but because the form in which they are pictured as happening is purely imaginary.

Anything Can Happen

The visionary strangeness of such writing leads to a related rule for reading it: *visionary literature is a form of fantasy literature in which readers must be willing to exercise their imaginations in picturing unfamiliar scenes and agents.* It requires what the poet Coleridge called "the willing suspension of disbelief." We know that people do not fly through the air on wings, but when reading such visions we suspend our disbelief and enter the realm of make-believe in order to appropriate the truth it conveys about reality. The best introduction to such visionary literature in the Bible is other fantasy literature, such as the Narnia stories of C. S. Lewis.

What is the point of such writing? Why would a biblical writer resort to fantasy instead of staying with realism? Visionary literature, with its arresting strangeness, breaks through our normal way of thinking and shocks us into seeing that things are not as they appear. Visionary writing attacks our ingrained patterns of deep-level thought in an effort to convince us of such things as that the world will not always continue as it now is, that there is something drastically wrong with the status quo, or that reality cannot be confined to the physical world that we perceive with our senses. Visionary

Visionary Literature as a Subversive Form

literature is not cozy fireside reading. It gives us the shock treatment.

Kaleidoscopic Structure

The element of the unexpected extends even to the structure of visionary literature. I will call it a kaleidoscopic structure. It consists of brief units, always shifting and never in focus for very long. Its effects are similar to those of some modern films. The individual units not only keep shifting, but they consist of a range of diverse material, including visual descriptions, speeches that the visionary hears and records, dialogues, monologues, brief snatches of narrative, direct discourses by the writer to an audience, letters, prayers, hymns, parables. Visionary elements, moreover, may be mingled with realistic scenes and events.

This disjointed method of proceeding places tremendous demands on the reader and is the thing that makes such literature initially resistant to a literary approach. The antidote to this frustration is a basic principle of interpretation: *instead of looking for the smooth flow of narrative, be prepared for a disjointed series of diverse, self-contained units.*

Dream Structure

Dream, and not narrative, is the model that visionary literature in the Bible follows. Of what do dreams consist? Momentary pictures, fleeting impressions, characters and scenes that play their brief part and then drop out of sight, abrupt jumps from one action to another. This is exactly what we find in visionary literature.

Pageant Structure

Sometimes, it is true, the units form a more discernible sequence than this, as in the visions of the four horsemen of Revelation (6:1–8). The model we should have in mind for such passages is the pageant—a succession of visual images that suggest in symbolic fashion an event or situation. In no case, however, does visionary literature in the Bible follow the typical structure of a story.

Narrative Elements

Even though visionary literature is not *structured* as a story, some of the standard narrative questions are exactly the right ones to ask. Individual units normally consist of the usual narrative elements of scene, agent, action, and outcome. The corresponding questions to ask of individual passages are:

1. *Where* does the action occur?
2. *Who* are the actors?
3. *What* do they do?
4. What is the *result*?

Not just the individual units but usually the books as a whole will yield some type of unity and organization if we ask these narrative questions:

1. What overall plot conflicts govern the work?
2. Who are the main actors in the work?
3. What changes occur as the book unfolds?
4. What final resolution is reached in regard to the overriding conflicts?

Symbolism as the Basic Mode

Visionary literature not only has story-like qualities; it makes even more use of the resources of poetry. And above all, visionary literature uses the technique of symbolism. In fact, it is symbolic through and through, a point that cannot be overstated. To insist that the Old Testament prophetic books and the Book of Revelation use symbolism as their basic mode is not to deny that they describe supernatural and historical events that really happen. The crucial question, however, is how the writers go about describing history.

The Reality of What Is Portrayed

It can be easily documented by ordinary historical means that the events described in visionary literature are historical in nature. For example, Israel and Judah *were* carried into captivity (as predicted in Old Testament prophecy), and the Roman Empire *did* fall (as predicted in Revelation). The literary question is, How are these historical realities portrayed in visionary literature? The answer usually is, By means of symbolism.

Symbolism in Old Testament Prophecy

Consider some typical specimens. The youthful Joseph dreamed that the sun, moon, and eleven stars bowed down to him. This symbolic picture was fulfilled later in his life, but the fulfillment was not literal. Isaiah described a river that overflowed the land of Judah. This symbolic picture was fulfilled historically (but not literally) when Assyria invaded and conquered Judah. The dream, interpreted by Daniel, of a statue composed of various minerals (Dan. 2:31–45) pictured historical realities, but it is not a literal description of those realities.

Symbolism in
the Book of
Revelation

The same type of symbolism prevails in the Book of Revelation. It is already present in the letters to the seven churches, the most realistic part of the whole book. We read, for example, about people "who have not soiled their clothes" (3:4) and who are destined to become "a pillar in the temple of my God" (3:12). Surely no one will interpret such statements literally. When the Christians at Laodicea are said to be lukewarm (3:16), we are obviously not talking about body temperature, and when they are described as being "poor, blind, and naked" (3:17) it is not a literal picture of their physical state but a symbolic picture of their spiritual condition. Nor does Christ literally stand at a physical door and knock (3:20). If there is this much symbolism already in the letters to the churches, how much more can we not expect in the futuristic sections of Revelation?

The action that unfolds in the opening verses of Revelation 12 is also a good index of the symbolic mode of the book. This passage narrates how a woman of cosmic dimensions (symbolic of Old Testament Israel) gives birth to a child "who will rule all the nations" (Christ), and it tells of the futile attempt of a great red dragon (Satan) to destroy the child, who is caught up into heaven. The most plausible interpretation of the passage is that it is a symbolic account of the incarnation and ascension of Jesus as narrated in the Gospels.

The corresponding question we need to ask of visionary literature in the Bible is a further principle of interpretation: *of what historical event or theological reality or event in salvation history does this passage seem to be a symbolic version?*

An example of a theological reality in symbolic form would be God's forgiveness of sins as seen in Zechariah's vision of the replacement of the high priest's filthy garments with clean ones (Zech. 3:3–5). Similarly, the sealing of believers in Revelation (7:2–3) is a symbolic picture of redemption. By "events in salvation history" I mean such events as the moral degeneration of the end times and the final judgment that are repeatedly pictured in the Book of Revelation.

We need to make a distinction between symbolic and pictorial effects. Visionary literature in the Bible is heavily symbolic but rarely pictorial. Many of the scenes in Revelation become grotesque the moment we visualize them as pictures. The portrait of Christ in Revelation 1:12–16, replete with a hand holding seven stars and a mouth with a sword issuing from it, is a series of symbols representing various aspects of Christ's character, not a composite picture of him. Someone has expressed the distinction thus:

> Symbolic writing. . .does not paint pictures. It is not pictographic but ideographic. . . .The skull and crossbones on the bottle of medicine is a symbol of poison, not a picture. . . .The fish, the lamb, and the lion are all symbols of Christ, but never to be taken as pictures of him. In other words, the symbol is a code word and does not paint a picture.[2]

How can we know what a given symbol means? It is relatively easy. In Old Testament prophecy the immediate context usually provides an interpretive framework for a given symbol or scene. Similarly, whenever a symbolic vision has been fulfilled in subsequent history, we can use that fulfillment to interpret the prophecy in which it was portrayed. This includes New Testament fulfillments of Old Testament prophetic and messianic visions.

A wide acquaintance with visionary literature both in the Bible and in literature generally is a great asset because literary symbolism tends to be a universal language that recurs throughout literature. Such common symbols as thunder, earthquake, dragon, lion, or harvest occur often enough in visionary literature for us generally to know what they mean.

Above all, we should never minimize the usefulness of contact with everyday experience and a keen eye for the obvious. The purpose of symbols

Visionary Literature Is Symbolic Rather Than Pictorial

Interpreting the Symbols

Symbols Are a Universal Language, Easily Grasped

A Keen Eye for the Obvious

---

[2]Donald W. Richardson, *The Revelation of Jesus Christ: An Interpretation* (Richmond: John Knox, 1939), 16. For convincing statements of the same viewpoint, see the excerpts under "Revelation, Book of, Symbolism," in *The New Testament in Literary Criticism*, ed. Leland Ryken (New York: Frederick Ungar, 1984).

is not to conceal but to reveal. A few of the symbols in the visionary literature of the Bible no doubt had a contemporary meaning that has been lost, but for the most part all we need is a sensitivity to the obvious associations of literary symbols. We do not need a commentary to tell us that a sword symbolizes judgment or a throne power or a vineyard prosperity.

Grasping the Total Meaning

Nor should we allegorize every detail in a passage unless there is a hint that we are intended to do so. Often it is the total impact of a scene or action that conveys the meaning.

The Mystery of the Supernatural

Then, too, some of the images portraying supernatural reality are meant to convey a sense of more-than-earthly mystery. Naturally, much remains elusive in Ezekiel's vision of the divine chariot (Ezek. 1). The images remain mysterious because their purpose is to convey the mystery of supernatural reality. Someone has contrasted the clarity of outline in Greek statues of the gods and the blurred edges of visionary writing in the Bible:

> The very clarity and definiteness of outline in those wonderful marbles stand out as a limitation: in comparison with these vague and mystical imaginings of the Christian seers the representations of Greek art are impotent. In the end the Greek statue of a god, for all its gracious beauty, is only a glorified and idealized man. The visions of the apocalypse, on the other hand, transcend once for all the limitations of human nature.[3]

SUMMARY

Visionary literature is what its name implies—an imagined picture, frequently symbolic rather than literal, of events that have not yet happened at the time of writing, or of realities such as heaven that transcend ordinary reality. Such writing requires that readers be ready to use their imagination—to let it fly beyond the stars. Visionary literature liberates us from the mundane and familiar and literal. It is an assault on our patterns of deep-level thought in an effort to shake us out of complacency with the normal flow of things. Visionary literature

---

[3]J. H. Gardiner, *The Bible as English Literature* (New York: Charles Scribner's Sons, 1906), 272.

is a revolutionary genre. It announces an end to the way things are and opens up alternate possibilities.

Further Reading

The characteristic rhetoric, imagery, and generic features of apocalyptic writing are discussed in these sources: William A. Beardslee, *Literary Criticism of the New Testament* (Philadelphia: Fortress, 1970), pp. 53–63; Amos N. Wilder, "Apocalyptic Rhetorics," in *Jesus' Parables and the War of Myths,* ed. James Breech (Philadelphia: Fortress, 1982), pp. 153–68; and vol. 14 of *Semeia* (1979), especially the introduction by John J. Collins (pp. 1–20).

For Old Testament prophecy, J. Lindblom, *Prophecy in Ancient Israel* (Philadelphia: Muhlenberg, 1962), is good on the visionary element (see especially pp. 122–82).

For literary commentary on the New Testament Book of Revelation, see the excerpts collected under that heading in *The New Testament in Literary Criticism,* ed. Leland Ryken (New York: Frederick Ungar, 1984); and my book *The Literature of the Bible* (Grand Rapids: Zondervan, 1974), pp. 335–56.

Chapter Twelve

The Literary Unity of the Bible

THE LITERARY RANGE AND DIVERSITY OF THE BIBLE are
truly impressive. Written by a variety of writers
over a span of many centuries, the Bible is an
anthology of literature, as the very name *Bible*
suggests (*biblia,* "books"). Previous chapters have
demonstrated how the list of biblical genres keeps
expanding. Every aspect of life is covered in this
comprehensive book. Because the Bible is both
comprehensive and written by a variety of writers,
it preserves the complexities and polarities of
human experience to an unusual degree. The
paradoxes of life are held in tension in what can be
called the most balanced book ever written. The
Bible is truly a book for all seasons and every
human temperament.

A Book for All
Seasons and
Temperaments

But if we stress only the variety of the Bible, we
distort the kind of book it is. For although the Bible
does justice to the breadth and fullness of human
experience in a marvelous way, it is also an
amazingly unified book. The purpose of this concluding chapter is to suggest some important ways
in which the Bible is *one* book. In keeping with the
literary focus of my book, I will be concerned
mainly with the *literary* unity of the Bible rather
than its theological unity.

The Literary
Unity of the
Bible

THE BIBLE AS A STORY

The most obvious element of literary unity in the
Bible is that it tells a story. It is a series of events
having a beginning, a middle, and an end. Even the

Narrative Unity
in the Bible

external shapeliness of the Bible is remarkable. It begins with the creation of all things. The story of the Fall quickly takes the action down to the level of fallen history. But the story slowly and painfully winds its way to the consummation of history with the eternal defeat of evil and the triumph of good.

The Unifying Plot Conflict

The overall story of the Bible has a unifying plot conflict. It is the great spiritual and moral battle between good and evil. A host of details makes up this conflict: God and Satan, God and his rebellious creatures, good and evil people, inner human impulses toward obedience to God and disobedience to God. Almost every story, poem, and proverb in the Bible contributes to this ongoing plot conflict between good and evil. Every act and mental attitude shows God's creatures engaged in some movement, whether slight or momentous, toward God or away from him.

The Prevalence of Human Choice

The presence of the great spiritual conflict makes choice on the part of biblical characters necessary. Every area of human experience is claimed by God and counterclaimed by the forces of evil. There is no neutral ground. Every human event shows an allegiance to God or rebellion against him. The Bible concentrates on the person at the crossroads. Life is momentous for the actors in this drama of the soul's choice. Viewed as a story, the Bible is a series of great moral and spiritual dilemmas and choices, underscoring the biblical view of people as morally responsible.

Human Choice, Not External Environment, Is Crucial

In the episodes that make up the overriding story of the Bible, the decisive action does not reside in external reality itself but consists of a person's *response* to what happens in the world. People's problems do not stem from outward events or the material world. Their moral and spiritual choices in history are the crucial action in the ongoing story of the Bible. Its plot is thus a moral/spiritual action in which external events provide *the occasion for* significant action, whether good or bad.

God as Protagonist

Every story has a central protagonist, and in the Bible that protagonist is God. He is the central character, the actor whose presence unifies the story of universal history with its myriads of changing human characters. Roland Frye comments:

> The characterization of God may indeed be said to be the central literary concern of the Bible, and it is pursued from beginning to end, for the principal character, or actor, or protagonist of the Bible is God. Not even the most seemingly insignificant action in the Bible can be understood apart from the emerging characterization of the deity. With this great protagonist and his designs, all other characters and events interact, as history becomes the great arena for God's characteristic and characterizing actions.[1]

It is obvious, then, that the chief element of progression in the overall story of the Bible is the unfolding purposes of God throughout history. Biblical scholars have taught us to call this "salvation history"—God's great plan to save people from their sin and its eternal consequences. The story of the Bible is the record of God's acts—in history, in nature, in the lives of people. Because it is God's purposes that comprise the essential action, the overriding story of the Bible can be called the history of the human race within a providential framework of God's acts of redemption from, and judgment against, the evil in the universe.

The Story of God

If we stand back from the Bible and take it in at a single view, it is above all a story, with many interspersed passages that interpret the meaning of the events. Like other stories, the Bible has a beginning–middle–end pattern, a unifying plot conflict between good and evil, a focus on people in the act of choosing, and a central protagonist who is God.

SUMMARY

THE RELIGIOUS ORIENTATION OF THE BIBLE

The Bible is also unified by its religious orientation. It is pervaded by a consciousness of God. Human experience is constantly viewed in a reli-

The Bible as a Religious Book

[1] Introduction to *The Bible: Selections from the King James Version for Study as Literature* (Boston: Houghton Mifflin, 1965), xvi.

gious or moral light. No matter how artistic and entertaining the Bible is, its writers have a didactic view of literature. Their purpose is to reveal truth to people so they can order their lives aright. Two oft-quoted descriptions of this aspect of the Bible are these:

> It is . . . not merely a sacred book but a book so remorselessly and continuously sacred that it does not invite, it excludes or repels, the merely aesthetic approach.[2]

> The Bible's claim to truth is not only far more urgent than Homer's, it is tyrannical—it excludes all other claims. The world of the Scripture stories is not satisfied with claiming to be a historically true reality—it insists that it is the only real world.[3]

The Theme of the Two Worlds

Part of the religious orientation of the Bible is the assumption of its writers that reality consists of two spheres. I call this the theme of the two worlds. Biblical writers take it for granted that there are two planes of reality—the physical world, perceived through the senses, and the supernatural world, invisible to ordinary human view. Both worlds are objectively real, but whereas earthly reality can be demonstrated empirically, the spiritual world must be accepted on faith. The constant appeal of biblical writers is for people to order their lives by the unseen spiritual realities, even though doing so usually contradicts earthly or human standards.

The Sense of Ultimacy

This transcendental stance of the Bible helps to produce two of its most constant and distinctive literary qualities. One is the sense of ultimacy with which the Bible invests human experience. What in most literature would be portrayed as a purely natural occurrence—the birth of a baby, a shower of rain, the daily course of the sun—is portrayed in the Bible as being rooted in a divine reality that lends spiritual significance to human and natural events. There is a continual penetration of the

---

[2]C. S. Lewis, *The Literary Impact of the Authorized Version* (Philadelphia: Fortress1963), 32–33.

[3]Erich Auerbach, *Mimesis: The Representation of Reality in Western Literature*, trans. Willard R. Trask (Princeton: Princeton University Press, 1953, 1968), 14–15.

supernatural into the earthly order. God is a continual actor in human affairs. The result is that life becomes filled with meaning, since every event takes on spiritual significance.

The supernatural slant of the Bible also produces a sense of mystery and wonder. By refusing to allow reality to be conceived solely in terms of known, observable reality, biblical literature continually transforms the mundane into something with sacred significance. As readers we are repeatedly confronted with a sense of the mystery of the divine beyond total human understanding. The Bible is a literature of mystery and wonder not because it conceals the spiritual but for precisely the opposite reason: it reveals the spiritual and thereby challenges the natural human tendency to explain life solely in earthly and natural terms.

The theme of the two worlds does not mean that biblical writers take historical reality any less seriously. On the contrary, they take it more seriously than is true of most of the world's literature. Biblical literature is firmly embedded in historical reality. It constantly claims to be history and has repeatedly been authenticated as history by modern archaeology. Compared with the fictional stories of modern writers, the storytellers of the Bible seem always to be eager to bring in historical facts. Snatches of historical chronicles, diaries, or genealogies are always creeping into the stories and poems of the Bible. Of course, the history of the Bible is not straightforward factual history. The historical facts are always presented within the interpretive framework of God's dealings with the human race.

The religious orientation of the Bible also includes the vivid consciousness of values that pervades it. Some conception of right and wrong underlies most literature, but in the Bible this conception is more sharply defined and more strongly held than elsewhere. For biblical writers the issue of what is good and evil is more important than anything else. Biblical authors are constantly saying, "This, not that." Biblical literature is similarly pervaded by a conviction that some things matter more than others. Ultimate value does not

The Mystery of the Supernatural

Preoccupation With History

Vivid Consciousness of Values

reside in anything or anyone apart from its relationship to God, nor can human endeavor be regarded as ultimately valuable apart from obedience to God. In the Bible, good and evil are supreme realities and are the most important issues in people's lives.

SUMMARY

One of the unifying elements in the Bible is its general sense of life. The prevailing attitude or perspective toward life throughout the Bible can only be called religious. It manifests itself most markedly in its awareness of supernatural reality and divine mystery, its conviction that human life in history is ultimately significant, and its vivid consciousness of values. These attitudes become the "air" within which biblical literature lives and moves and has its being.

UNIFYING THEMES

Unity of Subject Matter

Any body of literature can achieve unity on the basis of its topics and themes. If individual writers and works share a common subject matter, the literature inevitably begins to create a unified impression in a reader's mind. This is exactly what happens in the Bible. Individual biblical writers tend overwhelmingly to be preoccupied with a core of shared concerns.

The Character of God

Dominating everything is *the character of God.* The question of what God is like underlies more biblical passages than does any other concern. The most customary way of answering the question in the Bible is by narrating what God has *done,* but the Psalms, Prophets, Gospels, and New Testament Epistles also contain many direct statements about who God *is* in his inner being. This theme of God's self-revelation is so pervasive in the Bible that nearly every passage will provide an answer to the overriding question, *What is God like?*

The View of People

Balancing this preoccupation with God is a constant concern with people. This is not surprising, because the subject of literature is human experience. Most works of biblical literature are an implied assertion about human nature and destiny. Repeated themes include the significance of the individual, the importance of the individual's relationship to God and society, the simultaneous physical and moral/spiritual make-up of people, moral responsibility, and the capacity to make moral and spiritual choices.

The corresponding questions to ask of the stories, poems, proverbs, and visions of the Bible include these: *according to this passage, what are people like? What are their longings and fears? What values (for example, home, wealth, nature, God) are most worthy and least worthy of human pursuit? How can a person achieve meaning and happiness in life?*

Usually the twin topics of God and people appear together in biblical passages, making the theme of *the divine-human relationship* one of the big ideas of the Bible. Roland Frye theorizes that

> the pervasive theme of the Bible is the interaction between individuals, societies, and God, and one of the pervasive purposes of the Bible is to derive out of these interactions a clarification of each of the constituent elements. Throughout it is assumed that man cannot understand himself apart from God. . . .[4]

The theme of the divine–human relationship means that the Bible is a continuous exploration of people's inescapable connections with deity and God's unrelenting interest in what people do. The most customary biblical way of portraying this relationship is the idea of covenant.

Biblical authors write in a painful awareness that the divine–human relationship has been disrupted. A literary scholar writes, "From the quantitative point of view, three central subjects emerge. . . . This threefold theme is the interest of God in man, the wrath of God, and the weakness or rather the wickedness of humanity."[5] This is similar to T. R. Henn's belief that "overriding all else" is "the problem, re-stated constantly and from many angles of experience, of evil and suffering."[6]

The Divine-Human Relationship

Human Evil and Suffering

[4]Roland Frye, *Introduction*, xvi.

[5]Howard Mumford Jones, "The Bible from a Literary Point of View," in *Five Essays on the Bible* (New York: American Council of Learned Societies, 1960), 52.

[6]*The Bible as Literature* (New York: Oxford University Press, 1970), 257.

The Acts of
God

Another topic that pervades the pages of the Bible is *the history of God's acts*—his dealings with individual people, with Old Testament Israel, with the New Testament church. G. Ernest Wright has popularized the concept of the acts of God as the unifying center of the Bible.[7] These acts fall mainly into the categories of creation, redemption or salvation, and judgment. The concept of salvation history (discussed above) is virtually synonymous with the theme of the acts of God. Whatever designation we use, the theme remains the purposes of God as they occur in history. The corresponding question to ask of a given biblical passage is, *What is the nature of God's acts? What does or did God do, and for what purpose?*

The Acts of
People

The concern with what God does is almost always accompanied in the Bible by the theme of what people do or ought to do. Human behavior is a constant subject of biblical literature. It tends to fall into the dual pattern of virtuous behavior and sinful behavior. The Bible moves between the poles of human waywardness and human virtue. Using the twin techniques of portraying negative examples of vice to avoid and positive examples of virtue to imitate, the Bible presents a unified moral vision. This ethical unity of the Bible pervades both the expository parts and the literary sections, where it is incarnated in human characters, whether they be people actually doing things or the speaker in a lyric poem expressing the inner weather of his feelings (which also have moral implications in the Bible). The unifying moral preoccupation in biblical literature makes these questions relevant to most biblical texts: *What is typical or characteristic of human behavior? How should people behave?* In the Bible, description of human behavior is combined with an evaluative bias in such a way as to leave the reader with a sense of moral duty—of how people ought to live. Ethical duty, moreover, is not pictured as self-exertion toward moral perfection but as submission to God's law or conformity to his character.

---

[7]See especially *God Who Acts: Biblical Theology as Recital* (Chicago: Henry Regnery, 1952).

Luther and the Reformers interpreted the Bible through a thematic grid of *law and gospel* that is still useful as a way of seeing the unity of the Bible. In this view, the message of a biblical passage is either law or gospel (or both). "Law" is anything that exposes human ruin through sin. "Gospel" refers to everything that displays people's restoration through faith in God's grace. To use Melanchthon's formula, "The law indicates the sickness, the gospel the remedy." When flexibly applied, this framework of human sinfulness and divine grace yields much. Of most biblical passages we can ask, *What does this text say about human sinfulness and/or God's grace?*

Law and Grace

The theme of *God's promises and their fulfillment* is also a controlling theme of the Bible. T. R. Henn speaks of the Bible's "two major symphonic movements of promise and fulfillment."[8] This pattern appears in many forms, small and big, but the most important example is the relationship between the Old Testament and the New. This relationship has been well summarized by H. H. Rowley: "The Old Testament continually looks forward to something beyond itself; the New Testament continually looks back to the Old. Neither is complete without something beyond itself."[9]

Promise and Fulfillment

The New Testament builds upon the Old, bringing anticipations to fruition. Northrop Frye describes this overarching pattern of promise and fulfillment:

Old and New Testaments

There is a very large number of these references to the Old Testament in the New: they extend over every book—not impossibly every passage—in the New Testament. . . .The general principle of interpretation is traditionally given as "In the Old Testament the New Testament is concealed; in the New Testament the Old Testament is revealed." Everything that happens in the Old Testament is a "type" or adumbration of something that happens

[8]Henn, *Bible as Literature,* 21. Walter C. Kaiser, Jr., *Toward an Old Testament Theology* (Grand Rapids: Zondervan, 1978), 20–40, elaborates the same theme.
[9]*The Unity of the Bible* (Philadelphia: Westminster, 1953), 99.

in the New Testament, and the whole subject is therefore called typology.[10]

The result is a book in which no part is wholly self-contained but instead carries echoes from many other parts.

Unity of Reference

The vast *system of interlocking references and allusions* is not confined to New Testament fulfillments of Old Testament foreshadowings. Biblical writers share a common framework of reference. They keep referring to the same core of faith events. These events make up the underlying story of the Bible and are arranged into the following sequence: Creation, Fall, Covenant (promises of God to the patriarchs and Israelite nation), Exodus (including Revelation at Mount Sinai and Conquest of Canaan), Israelite Monarchy, Exile and Return, Life and Teaching of Jesus, Salvation (accomplished by the Death and Resurrection of Jesus), the Beginnings of the Christian Church, Consummation of History. This outline can be either expanded or telescoped. Northrop Frye divides the biblical story into seven "phases of revelation": Creation, Revolution, Law, Wisdom, Prophecy, Gospel, Apocalypse.[11]

This outline by itself imposes a loose unity on the Bible, but a much greater degree of cohesion results from the way in which biblical writers so consistently refer to this overriding story and its accompanying doctrines. No other long book in the world contains the interlocking system of references that have been codified in modern Bibles with cross references in the margins.

Unity of Faith

There is, finally, a *unity of faith* that welds the Bible into an organic whole. The Bible is not a theological outline, but the ideas that are stated and embodied in the Bible add up to a coherent system of doctrine. This doctrinal framework is a unifying context within which we should read individual parts. Everywhere we turn in the Bible, it is the same God and the same view of people that we encounter. The physical world is not considered good in one biblical book and evil in another. Of

[10]*The Great Code: The Bible and Literature* (New York: Harcourt Brace Jovanovich, 1982), 79.
[11]Ibid., 105–38.

course, no single passage by itself "covers the whole territory" on a given topic. Individual parts of the Bible are interdependent. When we put the parts together, we find a coherent set of doctrines whose main tenets include consistently held views about God, the nature of people, creation (nature, the physical world), providence, God's revelation as the source of truth, good and evil, salvation, and eschatology.

SUMMARY

As we read the Bible, we continually encounter a core of topics and themes. They include the character and acts of God, human nature and activity, moral good and evil, law and grace, promise and fulfillment. Biblical writers frequently refer to the same events that make up biblical history, and they share a common set of religious beliefs.

LITERARY ARCHETYPES IN THE BIBLE

A Definition of Archetypes

Literature is a great interlocking system in which we are continuously reminded of characters, situations, and symbols that we have encountered in other works of literature. These recurrent units are called *archetypes*. They fall into three categories: *images* (such as light, mountaintop, or prison), *character types* (such as the hero, villain, or tempter), and *plot motifs* (such as the quest, fall from innocence, or rescue). Archetypes are the basic building blocks of the literary imagination. When we read literature we are constantly in touch with them. Of course they recur in literature because they are pervasive in life. In both literature and life, archetypes elicit powerful universal responses from the human psyche.

A Pattern of Opposites

Archetypes tend overwhelmingly to fall into a pattern of opposites. We can label the two categories wish and nightmare, or the ideal and unideal, or the good and the evil. Together they are a vision of the kind of world that people want and do not want. The following table lists the most important archetypal images and character types in the Bible, arranged according to the dialectical pattern of opposites.

The Archetypes of Ideal Experience

The supernatural: God; angels; the heavenly society.

Human characters: the hero or heroine; the virtuous wife / husband / mother / father; the bride / groom; the innocent child; the benevolent king or ruler; the priest; the wiseman; the shepherd; the pilgrim.

Human relationships: the community, city, or tribe; images of communion, order, unity, friendship, love; the wedding or marriage; the feast, meal, or supper; the harmonious family; freedom; covenant, contract, or treaty.

Clothing: any stately garment symbolizing legitimate position or success; festal garments such as wedding clothes; fine clothing given as gifts of hospitality; white or light colored clothing; clothing of adornment (such as jewels); protective clothing such as a warrior's armor.

The human body: images of health, strength, vitality, potency, sexual fertility (including womb and seed); feats of strength and dexterity; images of sleep and rest; happy dreams; birth.

Food: staples such as bread, milk, and meat; luxuries such as wine and honey; the harvest of grain.

Animals: a community of domesticated animals, usually a flock of sheep or herd of cattle; the lamb; a gentle bird, often a dove; a faithful domesticated animal or pet; any animal friendly to people; singing birds; animals or birds noted for their strength, such as the lion or eagle; fish.

Landscape: a garden, grove, or park; the mountaintop or hill; the fertile and secure valley; pastoral settings or farms; the safe pathway or easily traveled highway.

Plants: green grass; the rose; the vineyard; the tree of life; any productive tree; the lily; evergreen plants (symbolic of immortality); herbs or plants of healing.

Buildings: the city; the palace or castle; the military stronghold; the tabernacle, temple, or church; the house or home; the tower of contemplation; the capital city, symbol of the nation.

The inorganic world: images of jewels and precious stones, often glowing and fiery; fire and brilliant light; burning that purifies and refines; rocks of refuge.

Water: a river or stream; a spring or fountain; showers of rain; dew; flowing water of any type; tranquil pools; water used for cleansing.

Forces of nature: the breeze or wind; the spring and summer seasons; calm after storm; the sun or the lesser light of the moon and stars; light, sunrise, day.

Sounds: musical harmony; singing; laughter.

Direction and motion: images of ascent, rising, height (especially the mountaintop and tower), motion (as opposed to stagnation).

The Archetypes of Unideal Experience

The supernatural: Satan; demons or evil spirits; evil beasts and monsters such as those in the Book of Revelation; pagan idols.

Human characters: the villain; the tempter or temptress; the harlot/prostitute; the taskmaster, tyrant, or oppressor (usually a foreign oppressor); the wanderer, outcast, or exile; the traitor; the sluggard or lazy person; the hypocrite; the false religious leader or priest; the fool; the drunkard; the thief.

Human relationships: tyranny or anarchy; isolation among people; images of torture (the cross, stake, scaffold, gallows, stocks, etc.), slavery, or bondage; images of war, riot, feud, or family discord.

Clothing: ill-fitting garments (often symbolic of a position that is usurped and not held legitimately); garments symbolizing mourning (such as sackcloth, rent garments, dark mourning garments); dark clothes; tattered, dirty, or coarse clothing; any clothing that suggests poverty or bondage; a conspicuous excess of clothing.

The human body: images of disease, deformity, barrenness, injury, or mutilation; sleeplessness or nightmare, often related to guilt of conscience; death.

Food: hunger, drought, starvation, cannibalism; poison; drunkenness.

Animals: monsters or beasts of prey; the wolf (enemy of sheep), tiger, dragon, vulture, owl (associated with darkness/ignorance), or hawk; the cold and earthbound snake; any wild animal harmful to people; the goat; the unclean animals of Old Testament ceremonial law.

Landscape: the dark forest; the wilderness or wasteland (which is either too hot or too cold); the dark and dangerous valley; the underground cave or tomb; the labyrinth; the dangerous or evil pathway.

Plants: the thorn or thistle; weeds; dead or dying plants; unproductive plants; the willow tree (symbolic of mourning).

Buildings: the prison or dungeon; the wicked city of violence, sexual perversion, or crime; the tower of imprisonment or wicked aspiration (the tower of Babel); pagan temples.

The inorganic world: the inorganic world in its unworked form of deserts, rocks, and wilderness; dry dust or ashes; fire that destroys and tortures instead of purifying; rust and decay.

Water: the sea and all that it contains (sea beasts and water monsters); stagnant pools (including the Dead Sea).

Forces of nature: the storm or tempest; the autumn and winter seasons; sunset, darkness, night.

Sounds: discordant sounds, cacophony, weeping, wailing.

Direction and motion: images of descent, lowness, stagnation or immobility, suffocation, confinement.

The Organizing Function of Archetypes

This chart of archetypes outlines the basic "language" of the literary imagination throughout the Bible. The list of images and character types is an organizing framework for the entire Bible. The unity of the Bible is partly a unity of master images.

The One Story of Literature

Archetypes can also consist of plot motifs. In fact, all of literature adds up to a single composite story known in literary circles as "the monomyth" (the "one story" of literature). The monomyth, which should not be confused with "mythology," is shaped like a circle and has four separate phases. As such, it corresponds to some familiar cycles of human experience. The cycle of the year, for example, consists of the sequence summer–fall–winter–spring. A day moves through a cycle consisting of sunrise–zenith–sunset–darkness. A person's life passes from birth to adulthood to old age to death. The monomyth, too, is a cycle having four phases.

We can picture the "one story" of literature like this:

Romance portrays idealized human experience—life as we wish it to be. Its opposite, anti-romance, pictures a world of bondage and misery. Tragedy narrates a fall downward from bliss to catastrophe, while comedy narrates a rise from bondage to happiness and freedom. These are the four kinds of literary material, and together they make up the composite story of literature. It is easy to see how the two categories of archetypal images and character types noted above make up the upper and lower halves of the monomyth.

The monomyth is the most general or universal pattern to be found in literature. The circular pattern of the monomyth takes a number of specific forms, including the following:

Archetypal Plot Motifs

1. *The quest,* in which a hero struggles to reach a goal, undergoing obstacles and temporary defeat before achieving success (Abraham's quest for a son and Ruth's quest for a home).

2. *The death-rebirth motif,* in which a hero endures death or danger and returns to life or security (the stories of Hezekiah and Jesus).

3. *The initiation,* in which a character is thrust out of an existing, usually ideal, situation and undergoes a series of ordeals as he or she encounters various forms of evil or hardship for the first time (the stories of Jacob and Joseph).

4. *The journey,* in which characters encounter danger and experience growth as they move from one place to another (the stories of Abraham and the Exodus).

5. *Tragedy,* or its more specific form of *the fall from innocence,* (the stories of Adam/Eve and David/Bathsheba).

6. *Comedy,* a U-shaped story that begins in prosperity, descends into tragedy, but rises to a happy ending as obstacles to success are overcome (the stories of Esther and Job).

7. *Crime and punishment* (the stories of Cain and King Saul).

8. *The temptation,* in which someone becomes the victim of an evil tempter or temptress (the stories of Eve and Samson/Delilah).

9. *The rescue* (the stories of Esther and of Elisha at Dothan).

10. *The suffering servant or scapegoat pattern,* in which a character undergoes unmerited suffering in order to secure the welfare of others (the stories of Joseph and Jesus).

Type Scenes

In addition to archetypal plot motifs, there are type scenes (not to be confused with types or typology) in the Bible. A type scene is a story pattern or situation that recurs often enough in the Bible that we can identify a set of conventions and expectations for each one. Each type scene has its constituent ingredients in an established order. An awareness of such type scenes can become a significant organizing pattern for either individual books of the Bible or the Bible as a whole.

Type Scenes in the Book of Acts

In the Book of Acts, for example, the following cycle of events keeps getting repeated: God raises up leaders who preach the Gospel; they perform mighty works; crowds are drawn and many hearers are converted; opposition and persecution arise against the leaders; God intervenes to rescue them; and on to a new reenactment of the cycle.[12] Other type scenes also unify the Book of Acts—preaching the gospel, conversion stories, and trial/defense scenes.

Such type scenes occur throughout the Bible. Robert Alter cites the Old Testament examples of "the annunciation . . . of the birth of the hero to his barren mother; the encounter with the future betrothed at a well; the epiphany in the field; the initiatory trial; danger in the desert and the discovery of a well or other source of sustenance; the testament of the dying hero."[13] The type scene that dominates the story of the Exodus is the situation that unfolds according to this sequence: crisis— complaint by the people—call to God by Moses— divine rescue/provision—revelation or rebuke by God. The Gospels have their distinctive type scenes: healing stories, pronouncement stories, preaching to the crowds, encounter stories, Passion stories. Each biblical type scene consists of a set of conventional elements, usually in a set order.

Type Scenes Throughout the Bible

The Bible is not a collection of isolated fragments. It is a vast system of recurring images, character types, plot motifs, and type scenes. As we read a given biblical passage, we are reminded of other similar material elsewhere in the Bible. In this process, the Bible assumes a remarkable unity in our thinking.

SUMMARY

UNIFYING STYLISTIC TRAITS

The Bible is written in a rich variety of styles. In the midst of all the variety, however, certain stylistic tendencies help to give the Bible a discernible literary unity. There are, of course, numerous passages that do not fit the generalizations I am about to note, but the very fact that we think of these as exceptions proves the validity of the

---

[12]M. D. Goulder, *Type and History in Acts* (London: S.P.C.K., 1964), organizes the entire Book of Acts around this type scene.

[13]*The Art of Biblical Narrative* (New York: Basic Books, 1981), 51.

general rules that scholars have attributed to the Bible's style.

Concrete Rather Than Abstract

The biblical tendency toward the concrete is well known. There are many great abstractions in the Bible (including the Psalms), but in general the biblical writers show a concern for things rather than ideas. God is portrayed as light and rock and thunder. Wealth is visible and tangible. So are human emotions. Even the prose sections of the Bible resemble poetry in their reliance on concrete images.

Realism

The Bible is a realistic book. Its characters and settings are predominantly nonaristocratic (unlike other ancient literature). The Bible, writes Erich Auerbach, "engenders a new elevated style, which does not scorn everyday life and which is ready to absorb the sensorily realistic, even the ugly, the undignified, the physically base."[14] The Bible also portrays the flaws of even its best characters.

Simplicity

The style of the Bible is marked by simplicity. Its characteristic imagery comes from daily life. Its narrative style is plain and unembellished, with only the essential details included. Shakespeare has a vocabulary of more than fifteen thousand words and Milton thirteen thousand, while the King James Bible has a vocabulary of about six thousand different words.[15] The biblical imagination also operates with simplified dichotomies, such as light and darkness, good and evil, heroes and villains, the tiny nation against its overpowering enemies. "The simplicity of the Bible," writes Northrop Frye, "is the simplicity of majesty. . . ; its simplicity expresses the voice of authority."[16]

Elemental Quality

The Bible is *par excellence* the book of elemental human experience. It depicts what is true for all people in all times and places. In the words of John Livingston Lowes, "the Biblical vocabulary is compact of the primal stuff of our common humani-

---

[14]*Mimesis*, 72.

[15]Cleland B. McAfee, *The Greatest English Classic* (New York: Harper and Brothers, 1912), 105.

[16]*The Great Code*, 211.

ty—of its universal emotional, sensory experiences.''[17] Someone else has expressed it thus:

> The themes of the Bible are simple and primary. Life is reduced to a few basic activities—fighting, farming, a strong sexual urge, and intermittent worship. . . .We confront basic virtues and primitive vices. . . .The world these persons inhabit is stripped and elemental—sea, desert, the stars, the wind, storm, sun, clouds, and moon, seedtime and harvest. . . . Occupation has this elementary quality also.[18]

Brevity

The Bible displays a preference for brevity over length. Biblical writers overwhelmingly work with brief units that are relatively self-contained. Individual episodes in stories from Genesis through the Gospels are almost never elaborated at length. The characters in these stories are illuminated by momentary flashes of heroism or evil or courage and so forth. When we move from the stories of the Bible to other genres, the forms are consistently brief ones: lyric, song, parable, proverb, prophetic vision, letter. The aphoristic, or proverbial, style of the Bible is a further evidence of this preference for conciseness and economy. The Bible is therefore a vast collection of concentrated moments of epiphany, "a series of ecstatic moments or points of expanding apprehension," as Northrop Frye calls it.[19]

Repetition

All of literature relies on various forms of repetition, but the Bible has even more of it than most literature, probably because so much of the Bible was originally oral literature. In poetry this urge for repetition takes the form of parallelism and rhetorical patterns. There is an equal abundance of repetition in the stories of the Bible, Jesus' parables and discourses, and the Epistles.[20]

---

[17]"The Noblest Monument of English Prose," in *Literary Style of the Old Bible and the New,* ed. D. G. Kehl (Indianapolis: Bobbs-Merrill, 1970), 9.

[18]Jones, "The Bible," 52–53.

[19]*Anatomy of Criticism* (Princeton: Princeton University Press, 1957), 326.

[20]Good sources to consult as a starting point on repetition include James Muilenburg, "A Study in Hebrew Rhetoric: Repetition and Style," *Vetus Testamentum Supplements* 1

196 HOW TO READ THE BIBLE AS LITERATURE

The Spoken Word

The style of the Bible is an oral style. The prevalence of dialogue in biblical narrative is unique in ancient literature.[21] But the Bible is everywhere filled with voices speaking and replying. To read the Bible well is to become a listener, either literally or in one's imagination.

Affective Power

The style of the Bible is predominantly *affective*. It moves us as well as appealing to our reason. It convinces us by evoking a response from us. The characteristic (though not exclusive) biblical way of conducting an argument is to repeat the main point so often that we *feel* or experience the truth of the assertion. The stories and parables of the Bible force us to respond to characters and events. The poems and oratory and Epistles are impassioned.

SUMMARY

The style of the Bible is uniquely powerful and beautiful. It can be parodied but never duplicated. The elements that make the Bible the most expressive book in the world include concreteness, realism, simplicity, an elemental quality, brevity, repetition, emphasis on the spoken word, and affective power.

Further Reading

The strength of Northrop Frye's *The Great Code* is the way in which it leaves a reader with a unified impression of the whole Bible. The best short introduction to the literary unity of the Bible is Roland M. Frye, "Introduction" to *The Bible: Selections from the King James Version for Study as Literature* (Boston: Houghton Mifflin, 1965; reprint, Princeton: Princeton University Press, 1977), pp. ix–xxxix. Volume 5 (1951) of *Interpretation* contains numerous still-useful articles on the unity of the Bible. The sources cited in the

---

(1953): 97–111; Robert C. Tannehill, *The Sword of His Mouth* (Philadelphia: Fortress, 1975); Jacob Licht, *Storytelling in the Bible* (Jerusalem: Magnes, 1978), 51–95; and Alter, *Art of Biblical Narrative*, 88–113.

[21]See Auerbach, *Mimesis*, 46; Alter, *Art of Biblical Narrative*, 63–87; and Amos N. Wilder, *Early Christian Rhetoric* (Cambridge: Harvard University Press, 1971), 40–54.

footnotes to chapter 12 also have good additional comments on the topic.

A wealth of good generalizations about the style of the Bible has been gathered by D. G. Kehl, ed., *Literary Style of the Old Bible and the New* (Indianapolis: Bobbs-Merrill, 1970).

Appendix:
The Allegorical Nature
of the Parables

The part of this book that will be most objectionable to biblical scholars is my discussion of the parables as allegories. It seems advisable, therefore, to explore the matter in more detail in this appendix.

The approach of biblical scholars is based from start to finish on their aversion (which I share) to the arbitrary allegorizing of the Bible that the medieval Fathers championed and that has been around ever since. For some people, moreover, the very concept of allegory has connotations of being simplistic or superficial (a bias that I do not share). Convinced that allegory is a bad thing, biblical scholars proceed to multiply the reasons why the parables cannot be considered allegorical. For the most part, these reasons betray an understanding of allegory that simply does not hold up when applied to literature in general.

I have outlined my own proposed solution in my chapter on the parables. I believe that it will only create confusion if we deny the name allegory to stories that fit the definition of allegory as applied elsewhere in literature. It is far preferable to treat the parables as allegorical texts and then to insist on accurate as opposed to arbitrary interpretation of the details. Allegorizing a biblical text is illegitimate, but interpreting an allegorical text is not.

I propose that we take a critical look at the reasons that are commonly offered for denying that the parables are allegorical. The list of such arguments includes the following.

The parables are not allegorical because in an allegory every detail has a corresponding "other" meaning. This is untrue of allegory in literature generally, where the same range exists as we find in the parables, as Northrop Frye suggests with his allegorical continuum. On the opening page of Bunyan's *Pilgrim's Progress,* for example, we attach allegorical meaning to such details as Christian, the book in his hand, and the burden on his back, but not to his house, wife, and children. When Aslan is killed near the end of C. S. Lewis's *The Lion, the Witch, and the Wardrobe,* we ascribe symbolic meaning to Aslan's death and resurrection, but not to such narrative details as the stone table, the shaving of Aslan, and the mice who gnaw through the ropes binding Aslan. It is a very rare exception, not the rule, to find allegories in which every detail has a corresponding meaning.

The parables are not allegories because "the details are not intended to have independent significance" (Charles Dodd). Modern scholarship has championed the view that we should ignore the individual details in the parables and stand back at such a distance from them that only one general point emerges. But this is something we cannot do even if we try because with most of the parables at least some of the details automatically remind us of a corresponding reality. Jesus himself provided the model for such interpretation. When Jesus interpreted the parable of the sower for his disciples (Matt. 13:18–23), he gave a corresponding meaning to every major detail in the story except the sower. When Jesus explained the parable of the wheat and the tares (Matt. 13:36–43), he gave eight of the narrative details a meaning.

Even Milton Terry, who denies that the parables are allegorical, admits that "most of the details in a parable have a meaning, and those which have no special significance in the interpretation serve, nevertheless, to enhance the force and beauty of the rest" (*Biblical Hermeneutics* [1883; reprint ed., Grand Rapids: Zondervan, 1964], 286). In my chapter on the parables I cited the conclusions of M. D. Goulder, who found that 82 percent of the details in the parables in Matthew's Gospel have a corresponding meaning, 75 percent in Mark, and 60 percent in Luke. Of course some parables (such as the parable of the good Samaritan) have no allegorical details. What we need, therefore, is a sliding scale that allows us to be flexible in describing the unique contours of each parable; Frye's allegorical continuum provides exactly this flexibility.

"The point of the parable is not in the points of reference as it would be in a true allegory" (Fee/Stuart). The mere identification of correspondences is never synonymous with the main theme or purpose of an allegory. Once we have identified Bunyan's City of Destruction as the lost state and the Slough of Despond as despair over one's sin, we must still translate those details into a statement of literary theme and purpose. If, on the other hand, the quoted statement means that the allegorical details in a parable are somehow extraneous to the theme of a parable, this, too, is untrue. In the parable of the prodigal son, for example, the whole point of the parable depends on our identifying the father as God, the prodigal as a repentant sinner, and the elder brother as the scribes and Pharisees.

"The parable uses words in their literal sense, and its narrative never transgresses the limits of what might have been actual fact. The allegory is continually using words in a metaphorical sense, and its narrative, however supposable in itself, is manifestly fictitious" (Terry,

p. 302). Here, too, the neat dichotomy between allegory and parable breaks down. The parables, for example, have struck most readers through the centuries as being "manifestly fictitious," a quality that Terry reserves for allegory. Allegory, says Terry, uses words "in a metaphorical sense." So do the parables; in fact, recent parable interpretation has stressed their metaphorical qualities. Many of the details in Jesus' parables already had metaphoric meanings before Jesus told them: God as father, judge, and vineyard owner; God's word as seed that is planted; divine judgment as a harvest—the list goes on and on.

It is true that the parables are noteworthy for the realism of their surface details, whereas most allegories have employed the techniques of fantasy part of the time (though rarely all of the time). But the narrative details of a work like *The Pilgrim's Progress* are often taken straight from Bunyan's local Bedfordshire. In any case, allegory *need* not be fantastic, as Jesus' allegory of the Good Shepherd (John 10:1– 18) illustrates. Besides, the parables of Jesus, for all their realism, are saturated with elements of the preposterous or exaggerated, such as a grain of wheat that when planted produces a hundred grains, a mustard plant treated as though it were a gigantic tree, an employer who completely disregards how long his employees have worked when he pays them, and a housewife who bakes a bushel of bread dough.

The parables are not allegories because in allegory the surface details of the story are unimportant in themselves and exist only to point to a truth beyond themselves. This may be true of transparent or unsophisticated allegory, but not of genuinely literary allegory. Allegories like Edmund Spenser's *Faerie Queene* or Bunyan's *Pilgrim's Progress* are literary masterpieces that elicit the reader's full imaginative response at the realistic or surface level of the narrative. Great literary allegory is bifocal, engaging a reader's interest at two levels (literal and allegorical) simultaneously. Literary allegory does not give us a simple one-for-one correspondence because surface details such as Bunyan's slough, journey, burden, and river are too connotative and multifaceted to be reduced to a single conceptual parallel. (For more on this subject, see E. Beatrice Batson's *John Bunyan: Allegory and Imagination* [London: Croom Helm, 1984].)

"A parable is aesthetic in a way that an allegory is not" (Dan Via, Jr.). For many scholars, this is really the heart of the matter: the parables are just too good to be allegorical! But literary classification should be descriptive, not honorific. Besides, modern criticism on such literary masterpieces as *The Divine Comedy*, *The Faerie Queene*, and *The Pilgrim's Progress* has long since exploded old myths about the supposed artistic anemia of literary allegory. (Here, too, Batson's book is the best source.)

When we look closely at what biblical scholars say, it is apparent to me that their comments misconstrue the nature of allegory as a literary form. If we apply the scholar's composite definition of allegory to literature as a whole, there is virtually no piece of literature to which we could apply the title.

The result of denying that the parables are allegorical has been to confuse people about how to deal with the parables. We are told that the parables are not allegories, and then we find Jesus allegorizing the parables of the sower and the wheat and tares. Nor does it inspire confidence in our ability to handle parables to be told that "the parables are not allegories—even if at times they have what appear to be allegorical features" (Fee/Stuart).

The most obvious feature of the parables is that they are realistic stories, simple in construction and didactic ("aiming to teach") in purpose, that convey religious truth and in which the details often have a significance beyond their literal narrative meaning. In any other context we would call such works allegorical. My proposal is simple and commonsensical: we should begin with what is obvious (that the parables tend to be allegorical) and *then* note those things that distinguish these particular allegories: their profound realism, their brevity, their absence of allegorical names for people and places, their persuasive strategy designed to force a response, their ingenious way of subtly undermining ordinary patterns of thinking, their variability in regard to how many details call for a corresponding meaning, and their artistic excellence.

Of course we need to insist on curbs to the interpretive process in order to eliminate arbitrary allegorizing of the medieval type. These curbs include the interpretive clues contained in the narrative links before or after a parable as it appears in the Gospel narratives; the traditional symbolic meanings of a given detail (especially if those meanings appear within the Bible itself); compatibility with the inferred purpose or main teaching of a parable; and compatibility with biblical/Christian doctrine. There must be a good reason drawn from the biblical text before we attach a given meaning to a detail in a parable. In keeping with the oral nature of the parables, a general or obvious meaning is truer to the spirit of a parable than a specific or obscure meaning. In a parable that teaches about stewardship (Matt. 25:14–30), for example, the money that is entrusted to the three stewards should be interpreted in general terms as a person's abilities, time, and opportunities, not specifically as the Holy Spirit. We must, in short, insist on *interpretation of allegorical details rather than arbitrary allegorizing,* but in the meantime we must not try to deny the obvious symbolic meanings in parables.

The academic world has surrounded the parables with so many intricate rules for interpreting them that ordinary people have become convinced that they had best leave the parables to the specialist. It is time to give the parables back to the group to which Jesus originally told them—ordinary people. Viewing the parables as allegorical would be a step in the right direction, since simple allegory has usually struck ordinary people as being accessible.

Index of Persons